From Colonies to Country
1735–1791

TEACHING GUIDE FOR THE
3RD EDITION

For Elementary School Classes

OXFORD
UNIVERSITY PRESS

Oxford University Press

Oxford   New York

Auckland   Bangkok   Buenos Aires
Cape Town   Chennai   Dar es Salaam   Delhi   Hong Kong   Istanbul
Karachi   Kolkata   Kuala Lumpur   Madrid   Melbourne   Mexico City   Mumbai
Nairobi   São Paulo   Shanghai   Singapore   Taipei   Tokyo   Toronto

and an associated company
Berlin

Published by Oxford University Press, Inc.
198 Madison Avenue, New York, New York 10016
Oxford is a registered trademark of Oxford University Press

ISBN 978-0-19-976736-6

Writer: Karen Edwards
Editor: Rosely Himmelstein
Editorial Consultant: Susan Buckley

Printed in the United States of America on acid-free paper

CONTENTS

NOTE FROM THE AUTHOR

Dear Teacher,

Every writer of history has to make decisions. Most of those decisions are about what to leave out. It would take libraries and libraries of books to include all of America's history (and there would still be things left out).

So there are all kinds of stories about America (and its heroes and villains and ordinary people) that are not in this book. I see that as an opportunity for you and your students. Tell them the author is upset about what she had to omit. Have them do their own chapters of *A History of US*. Maybe you can do a class volume. Consider focusing on family stories: what can each of your students find out about his or her ancestors? Or maybe you'll want to do a book about your community with chapters on people and organizations and past events.

I have fun tracking down stories; I think you and your students will, too. (Yes, I hope you'll become a student with them.) Writing history is a lot like being a detective or a newspaper reporter. It involves searching for information, digesting it, and then using it. There are hardly any better skills for this Information Age of ours.

You and your students might want to find out more about Indians— especially the Native Americans in the region where you live. Or more about Coronado, or Ben Franklin, or about Americans not even mentioned in these books. Good writers look for details. Check paintings and photographs. What does your subject look like? How did he or she dress? What was daily life like for that person?

You might want to produce the work in comic book form, or write it as a play, or create a ballad. The big idea here is to "do" history, as you might do art or music. At its best, it's a creative activity.

But the big reason I wrote these books was to teach reading and, when it comes to critical reading, history shines. Few subjects give you real events and real people to discuss and analyze. Literacy exercises and paragraph analysis may help some students, but there is nothing like reading a whole book—tracing its ideas from chapter to chapter, and then talking about the ideas—to make a mind work.

This learning guide has words to study and maps to look at and questions to answer. You may want your students to do all the activities, or you may want them to do just a few. Some activities are for those who want to go beyond the text.

Will all this help students pass standardized tests? You bet. Just to be sure, though, I have added some pages with names and dates that you may ask students to memorize.

But there are things in history more important than memorized dates. History is a thinking subject, and you have Information Age kids as your charge. Doing history means reading, researching, finding information, and making connections. If you want to stretch young minds, history will make it happen.

Joy Hakim

ABOUT THIS TEACHING GUIDE

*A*History of US* is the story of what happened in the United States to the
people who live here—both before and after the country got its name.
In *From Colonies to Country*, students will learn what happened between
1735 and 1791. This teaching guide, containing strategies and assessment
suggestions as well as a range of activities for enrichment and extension,
was prepared to help you guide your students through the book.

FOCUSING ON FREEDOM

The cornerstone of American history is Freedom. It is the idea that pulsates
throughout *A History of US*: the hunger for freedom, the fight for freedom,
the legislating of freedom, the protection of freedom, the defense of freedom. As you teach this volume of *A History of US*, students will learn how
the accomplishments of people, the force of ideas, and the outcome of
events are all linked in this nation's great story of Freedom.

A lot happens: sad, exhilarating, unexpected, disappointing, terrible,
puzzling, inspiring things. And many people are involved: the wise, the mis-
guided, the brave, the reckless, the patient, the bullies, the compromisers.
It's a grand and sweeping story.

May you and your students enjoy it together.

THE TEACHING UNITS

Each book of *A History of US* has been divided into units of study that we
call Parts. Each Part consists of chapters that have a common focus. The
Teaching Guide provides strategies and activities that you can use to teach
each Part.

- **Part 1: The Seeds of Conflict** (Chapters 1-6) focuses on the French and
  Indian War.

- **Part 2: Blazing New Trails** (Chapters 7-10) focuses on styles of
  American life and the origin of constitutional rights.

- **Part 3: The Sparks of War** (Chapters 11-15) focuses on colonial
  resistance leading to the Revolution.

- **Part 4: The Road to Independence** (Chapters 16-21) focuses on the
  Second Continental Congress and the Declaration of Independence.

- **Part 5: Fighting the War** (Chapters 22-28) focuses on men and women
  who fought the war.

- **Part 6: Experiments with Independence** (Chapters 29-34) focuses on
  the end of the war and building a nation.

- **Part 7: Creating a New Nation** (Chapters 35-42) focuses on creating the
  Constitution.

ORGANIZING INFORMATION

The history of the United States is rich, busy, and populated. You can help your students organize information and reinforce learning by frequently asking these questions:

- What were the major events?

- Who were the significant people?

- What were the important ideas?

Question Chart In every lesson plan, you will see a reference to the Question Chart (Resource 1, TG page 72), on which students may record their answers to these questions as they progress through the book.

THE BIG THEMES

Underlying the events and people and ideas that enliven this series are certain themes—themes that run through human experience and help us make sense of the past.

Among these themes are Justice, Conflict, Independence, Change, Diversity, Adaptation, Growth, and Power. You may wish to post these themes on the walls of your classroom and refer to them at appropriate times. They may also stir students' thinking throughout the course of their study.

Book 3 of *A History of US* focuses on two Big Themes: **Conflict** and **Change.** These themes—and how they relate to this nation's quest for and preservation of freedom—provide the conceptual framework of *From Colonies to Country.*

Among the major conflicts in the period 1735-1791 are:

- conflicts among European colonial powers over territory in North America.

- conflicts between Native Americans and colonists.

- conflicts between the ideas of monarchy and democracy.

- conflicts between Loyalists and Patriots.

- conflicts among delegates at the Continental Congress.

- conflicts over the relationship between the states and the central government.

Among the dramatic changes occurring in the period 1735-1791 are:

- change in the balance of power among colonial powers in North America.

- change in the attitude of American colonists toward Great Britain.

- change in the boundaries of lands settled by colonists.

- change in the relationship of the colonies to one another.

- change in the relationship of the colonies to Great Britain.

TEACHING STRATEGIES

The Teaching Strategies in this guide are organized in the following manner:

Introducing the Part lays out goals for teaching, sets up a relationship between the Part and the major themes, and seeks to stimulate students' interest as they begin to read the text.

Chapter Lesson Plans are designed to provide you with the flexibility that your individual schedule, interests, and students' abilities may require. You may choose from the following categories:

- **Ask:** straightforward questions to elicit from your students responses that demonstrate their recall and understanding of the text.

- **Discuss:** critical thinking questions to stimulate classroom and/or small-group discussions.

- **Write:** topics for classroom or homework assignment, allowing students to express their comprehension or impressions of the chapter's events, ideas, or people.

- **Ponder:** questions that give students the opportunity to reflect on the thematic material of the chapter, often relating it to their own lives.

- **Literacy Links:** *Words to Discuss,* exploring the chapter's significant vocabulary words or terms, and *Reading Skills* designed to help students develop reading skills, especially for reading nonfiction.

- **Skills Connection:** chapter-related activities to strengthen geography skills, chart/graph skills, study skills, and cross-curricula skills.

- **Meeting Individual Needs:** activities that address the needs of students with differing learning abilities.

Which of these categories will be suitable for your students on any particular day? How many items will be useful to engage your class—or a particular student? The lesson plans have been structured with the belief that *you* are the best person to make these decisions.

Summarizing the Part provides guidance for synthesizing the Part's Big Themes. This guidance consists of a series of questions—which you can use for assessment or discussion—that enable students to deepen their understanding of how the events, ideas, trends, and personalities of the Part reflect common themes. The Part Summary also provides additional Projects and Activities.

PART CHECK-UPS

The reproducible Check-Ups review the content of each Part.

RESOURCES

The Resources are reproducible blackline masters. They cover social studies skills (including maps, graphic organizers, tables, primary sources, and other enrichment materials), critical thinking skills, and reading comprehension skills.

LITERACY AND *A HISTORY OF US*

In our Information Age, reading is an essential survival skill. So what does this have to do with us historians and history educators? We have the key to the nation's reading crisis, and we've been ignoring it: When it comes to critical reading, history shines. Hardly anything approaches it in its demands for analysis and thinking.
Joy Hakim

Teaching with *A History of US* gives you an unparalleled opportunity to focus on literacy. As the author has noted, "Nonfiction is the literary form of our time." Joy Hakim's highly readable nonfiction is a unique tool for teaching strategic reading skills.

READING STRATEGIES AND SKILLS

In order to help your students get the most out of their reading, the Teaching Guides include activities that focus on reading skills as well as reading strategies.

Reading Skills deal with what students actively do with the nonfiction text. The Reading Skills activities in the chapter lesson plans help students identify, evaluate, interpret, understand, and use the following nonfiction elements:

- Text Structure: main idea/supporting details, sequence, comparing and contrasting, question and answer, cause and effect

- Text Features: margin notes, special sections, captions, headings, typeface

- Visual Aids: photographs, paintings, illustrations, political cartoons

- Graphic Aids: graphs, tables, charts, timelines

- Maps: political, physical, historical, special purpose

- Point of View: author's voice and opinion

- Source Material: primary and secondary sources

- Rhetorical Devices: word choice, imagery, connotation/denotation, persuasion, fact and opinion, analogy

Reading Strategies are the intellectual strategies necessary for readers to use their reading skills. Following the ideas of reading authority Janet Allen, these can be categorized as follows:

- Questioning: creating questions to aid with previewing, recalling, and deeper understanding of the text

- Predicting: focusing and guiding reading by previewing text elements and posing questions to be answered

- Visualizing: identifying and using language and imagery to infer, make connections to the text, and predict

- Inferring: identifying text clues and background knowledge to make inferences; using inferences to make predictions and draw conclusions

- Connecting: making personal connections to the text, seeing connections between texts, seeing connections between world events and the text

- Analyzing: recognizing the relationship between author's intention and author's words, determining author's purpose, understanding how parts of the text work together, using material from the text to support response to the text

- Synthesizing: creating an original idea, new line of thinking, or other new creation by combining related ideas

Each Reading Skill activity is related to one of the Reading Strategy categories.

NOTE You probably present material to your students in a variety of ways. There are times you may read aloud to the class or in small groups. Perhaps you'll find it best to have volunteers read aloud—or have the class read silently. You'll find that *A History of US* allows you to vary your approach to suit your schedule and your goals.

LITERACY HANDBOOK: *READING HISTORY*

Reading History is written by Janet Allen, one of American's most prominent literacy advocates. Engaged in the blossoming campaign to integrate literacy and history, Allen provides valuable strategies for teaching nonfiction, taking all examples directly from *A History of US*. Allen says:

> For the past several years, many content teachers have voiced a common complaint: As we teach and learn with a generation of children who have been raised on technology and sophisticated media, it becomes increasingly difficult to entice them into reading content textbooks. Reading History *has been written to help you teach your students effective strategies for reading* A History of US *as well as other nonfiction. It is filled with practical ideas for making reading history accessible for even your most reluctant readers.*

ASSESSMENT AND *A HISTORY OF US*

Author Joy Hakim intentionally omits from her books the kinds of section, chapter, and unit questions that are used to review and assess learning in standard textbooks. It is her purpose to engage readers in learning—and loving—history. Rather than interrupt student reading, all assessment instruments for *A History of US* appear in the Teaching Guides.

IN THE TEACHING GUIDES

Ask, Discuss, and Write sections in each chapter lesson plan check students' understanding of chapter content.

Summarizing the Part includes questions for discussion or writing, and activities that help students identify major concepts and themes.

Check-Up pages review content for each Part. These are reproducible pages that appear at the end of each Teaching Guide.

HISTORICAL OVERVIEW

Patriots attack a Loyalist

When in the Course of human events it becomes necessary for one people to dissolve the political bands which have connected them with another . . .

With these words, the Declaration of Independence announced the severing of ties between the American colonies and Great Britain. It was a separation that came about after decades of conflict between the colonists and the English government. By 1776 the colonists decided to go it alone rather than submit to the oppression of a government that would not grant them the rights of other English people.

Since the founding of the Massachusetts Bay colony, the colonists had gained only a few freedoms. The trial of Peter Zenger in 1735, for example, helped established freedom of the press, freedom of speech, and trial by jury in the colonies.

In the 1750s and 1760s, the colonists' attitudes toward the home country started to change. Instead of trying to gain that same rights as people in England while remaining loyal to the English government, the colonists questioned the policies underlying colonialism itself.

John Adams believed the start of the American Revolution began with the French and Indian War. So do many historians. Britain's victory in 1763 solidified its power over the colonies. After its victory, Great Britain passed a series of laws and taxes in an effort to force the colonists to share the costs of the empire. This effort angered the colonists, who did not want to be ruled by an uncaring government thousands of miles away.

In the 1760s colonists organized to try to resist unfair British laws and taxes. At first, few colonists thought of separating altogether from Great Britain. But the British refused to compromise with the colonists, which only made the colonists angrier. Finally, in 1775, tempers snapped at Lexington and Concord, Massachusetts. Patriots (colonists) and redcoats (British soldiers) began killing each other. Shortly thereafter, the Second Continental Congress met in order to define the conflict. Most delegates did not want to break with Britain, but Patriots and redcoats kept killing each other. It was war.

Thomas Jefferson wrote the Declaration of Independence to win support for the Patriot cause both in the colonies and in England. The British government responded by trying to crush the rebels. The Revolutionary War was on.

When the war ended in 1781, the colonists faced a huge task. Needing to set up their own government, colonial leaders began a flurry of writing constitutions—both for their separate colonies or states as well as for the new federal government. They took ideas from English laws, the Iroquois Federation, and the Enlightenment and put them into practice. They also created some uniquely American principles of government, such as separation of church and state.

Today, the Constitution of the United States is the world's oldest working written plan of government. The events leading to the creation of this document form the story of Book Three of *A History of US.*

Battle of Bunker Hill

TEACHING STRATEGIES FOR BOOK THREE

The Seeds of Conflict

Long before shots rang out at Lexington and Concord, the forces of conflict and change had begun to alter the hearts and minds of Americans. In 1808, John Adams reflected on the events leading up to the American Revolution: "The radical change in the principles, opinions, and sentiments of the people was the real American Revolution." Part 1 tells us about how those changes began.

SETTING GOALS

The goals for students in Part 1 are to:
- understand the conflict between colonial powers in North America.
- explain how the French and Indian War changed the political landscape of North America.
- identify and describe the sources of the conflict that arose between England and its North American colonies.
- identify the roles of the key figures in the conflict.

GETTING INTERESTED

1. Write the title of Part 1 on the chalkboard. Ask: What are seeds and what do they do? *(They are very small things from which—over time—larger things grow.)* Why do you think the author uses the word *seeds* in relation to conflict? *(Help students see that in this story, small disagreements will grow into major disputes.)*

2. Have students turn to the poem on page 5 (opposite the copyright page). Have volunteers read the poem aloud. Ask: Who is the "old lady"? *(England)* Who is the "daughter"? *(the colonists)* What is the conflict between them about? *(a tax on tea)* How does the "daughter" rebel? *(She throws the tea into the ocean.)* Direct students to read the Preface to learn more about what led the people in the book to try to change things.

 Working with Timelines
Have students construct a timeline running from 1735 to 1791 on which they will record significant events and dates. (This can be an individual or a class activity.) The timeline can be divided into intervals chosen by the students. Students should take notes as they read and enter important dates on the timeline after each chapter.

 Using Maps
Have students turn to the world map on page 210, and locate England (United Kingdom). Ask them to use the scale to calculate the approximate distance between England and its colonies in North America. Elicit the kinds of problems that could occur between rulers and subjects who lived that far from each other.

Freedom of the Press

This chapter describes the trial of Peter Zenger and his successful defense by Andrew Hamilton, which established freedom of speech, freedom of the press, and trial by jury in the American colonies.

ASK

1. Why was Peter Zenger put in jail? *(He printed a newspaper with articles that criticized Governor William Cosby. He refused to stop publishing them.)*

2. What crime did the government charge Zenger with? *(libel, which is knowingly publishing lies about someone that hurt the person)*

3. What two arguments did Andrew Hamilton make at Zenger's trial? *(Free people have the right to tell the truth in print; a jury has the right to decide whether or not a crime has been committed.)*

4. What was the outcome of Zenger's trial? *(The jury found him not guilty.)*

 **Ponder**
Can you think of an instance when a person might believe so strongly in something that he or she would risk going to jail?

DISCUSS

1. Why did the jury agree with Andrew Hamilton and not the attorney general? *(The jury agreed that Zenger was publishing the truth. The articles may have hurt Governor Cosby, but the truth is not libel.)*

2. Why might British officials oppose freedom of the press among the colonists? *(The British wanted to keep the colonies under control; they didn't want the ideas of discontented colonists to spread.)*

3. Why was the Zenger case important to all the colonists? *(It allowed them to voice and publish opinions that were contrary to the official government opinion. It established that a jury, or group of citizens, could participate in a trial, so that the judge, who was a government official, could not abuse his powers.)*

✔️ **Question Chart**

WRITE

Have students imagine that they are living in the colonies in 1736. Ask them to write a letter to a relative in England, trying to persuade the person to move to America. The rights obtained as a result of the Zenger trial should be included in their arguments.

L I T E R A C Y   L I N K S

Words to Discuss

apprentice   libel
disbarred   arbitrary
indentured servant

Have students use a dictionary to find which word comes from a Latin word meaning "little book." *(libel)* Ask: Which two words have prefixes? *(disbarred, indentured)*

Reading Skills
Analyzing Rhetorical Devices

Have students list on the board *loaded words* (words with positive or negative connotations that stir strong emotions) from Hamilton's speeches at Zenger's trial. *(free men, oppose arbitrary power, truth, blessings of liberty, cause of liberty)* Have students discuss the effect such words might have had on the jury. VISUALIZING

Skills Connection
Fine Arts

Refer students to the picture of the print shop on page 14. Explain that it shows newspaper pages being "set by hand." Printers would place metal type letter by letter and space by space into a form from which an entire page would be printed. This painstaking process was not replaced until the early 20th century with the advent of the Linotype machine, which automated the job. Have students look up more information about the history of printing in a classroom encyclopedia.

Jenkins' Ear

When the Spaniards cut off Robert Jenkins' ear, war was the result. The issue was not Jenkins' ear, but control of North America.

ASK

1. What were the 18th-century wars amongst European countries about? *(The wars were about land, money, and economic gain.)*
2. What did the Spaniards do to Robert Jenkins? Why? *(They cut off one of his ears because they caught him smuggling slaves onto a Caribbean island they controlled.)*
3. How did the English react to this? *(They used what happened to Jenkins as an excuse to start war with Spain.)*
4. What were the results of the war for the English, Spanish, and colonists? *(The English and Spanish fought to a draw. The colonists began to be called "Americans" by the British, indicating new respect.)*

Ponder
Why do countries fight over land?

✔ Question Chart

DISCUSS

1. Why do you think the English began to call the colonists *Americans*? How did this affect the colonists? *(The English began to respect the colonists for their help in the war. The colonists were proud to be recognized as a separate people.)*
2. What was the real conflict in the war? *(control of land in North America)* Was the conflict resolved by the war? Why or why not? *(No; England, France, and Spain all still had colonies in North America.)* What do you predict will happen? *(There will be more wars.)*

WRITE

Ask students to write an editorial defending one of these points of view: "The War of Jenkins' Ear should have been fought" or "The War of Jenkins Ear should not have been fought." Encourage the use of facts and persuasive techniques in students' writing.

L I T E R A C Y   L I N K S

Words to Discuss

people's war

Discuss the definition provided on page 17. Ask students if they can think of any examples of people's wars.

Reading Skills
Making Inferences

Have students read page 18 to learn about the clash between the colonies of Georgia and Florida. Discuss Oglethorpe's decision to take the offensive against the Spanish. Ask: What advantage did he seem to have? *(Native American allies, a British fleet)* What inference can you make about Oglethorpe's character? *(He was bold, courageous, a good leader.)* INFERRING

Skills Connection
Geography/Science

Yellow fever was a more potent killer than bullets in the War of Jenkins' Ear. Have volunteers use the Internet or classroom encyclopedias to research yellow fever, its causes and effects, and why it is linked to subtropical and tropical climates like that of Florida.

Frenchmen and Indians

The next colonial conflict in North America was between the British and the French. It was a struggle to control the land north and west of the Appalachian Mountains. Things did not go well for the British at first.

ASK

1. What claims did France and England have to the land west of the Appalachians? *(French explorers had been the first Europeans in the region; the charters for the English colonies granted them the land from coast to coast.)*

2. What did the French and English want from this land? *(The French wanted to profit from trade and furs; the English wanted to settle on the land.)*

3. What battle began the French and Indian War in 1754? What happened? *(George Washington and 150 men attacked a French scouting party. Then Washington built Fort Necessity, but the French captured the fort.)*

4. Why did the English lose the battle of Fort Duquesne in 1755? *(The French and Indians fought from behind rocks and trees, confusing and panicking the English.)*

◎ Ponder
Could the Indians have resisted the frontier people if they had united? For how long?

✓ Question Chart

DISCUSS

1. How was the relationship between the French and the Indians different from the relationship between the English and the Indians? *(The French understood the Indians' ways—they traded, trapped, fished, and respected the land. The English just wanted to take the land from the Indians—they broke treaties and had a very different idea about owning the land.)*

2. The French have won so far. Do you think they will win in the end? Why or why not? *(Students should discuss fighting tactics and the author's hint on page 23 that the powerful Iroquois will turn the tide against the French.)*

WRITE

Ask students to write a diary entry that Daniel Boone might have written after Braddock's defeat. They should describe what Boone saw and what he thought.

LITERACY LINKS

Words to Discuss

treaty **charter**

Have students use a dictionary to find the meanings of these words. Have them discuss how the meanings are similar and different. *(Both words refer to governmental documents; a charter describes rights that a government gives to people, whereas a treaty is an agreement between nations.)*

Reading Skills
Comparing and Contrasting

Have students complete a two-column chart contrasting the British/American forces with the French/Indian forces in clothing, use of the environment, tactics, and results. CONNECTING

Meeting Individual Needs
Visual Learners

Students may benefit by listening to the text description of Washington's defeat at Fort Necessity and Braddock's defeat at Fort Duquesne. Then have students draw scenes to illustrate those battles. Students' drawings might be assembled into a class book entitled *British Forces Learn the Hard Way.*

A Most Remarkable Man

An amazing English settler named William Johnson had the confidence of both English and Indians. Called *Warraghiyagey* by his Mohawk friends, he helped turn the course of the French and Indian War in favor of the British.

ASK

1. What key things did William Johnson do after he arrived in Albany? *(He learned the ways and language of the Mohawks. He became friends with Tiyanoga. He was named a Mohawk. He treated all people well.)*
2. What did the colonial leaders hope to accomplish at the Albany Congress? *(They wanted the colonies to form a union within the British empire—a colonial nation—and they hoped to get the Iroquois to help them fight the French.)*
3. What convinced the Iroquois to fight on the side of England and the colonists? *(Warraghiyagey called a council of the Iroquois League and promised the Indians that their land would be protected.)*
4. What was the outcome of the Battle of Lake George? *(Johnson and his troops and the Iroquois defeated the French under Baron Dieskau.)*

DISCUSS

1. Do you think the Mohawk name *Warraghiyagey* fits William Johnson? Why? *(The name means "he who does much," and it fits Johnson because he did many things for both Native Americans and European Americans. Students should mention some of his achievements.)*
2. Why did Benjamin Franklin admire the Iroquois form of government? *(The Iroquois had united six tribes into a confederation. By organizing separate states into one governmental system, the Iroquois became strong.)*
3. Why do you suppose the colonies would not ratify the Albany Plan of Union? *(They did not trust each other. Elicit that each colony was like its own country, with few ties to the other colonies.)*

WRITE

Ask students to write a brief character sketch of William Johnson, including the qualities and accomplishments that helped make him a subject for history books.

L I T E R A C Y   L I N K S

Words to Discuss

confederation	sachem
feudal lord	baronet

Have students use a dictionary as well as context to determine the meanings of the words. Discuss: Which three words have something in common? *(feudal lord, sachem, baronet: all concern nobles or leaders)*

Reading Skills
Analyzing Cartoons

Draw students' attention to the "Join or Die" political cartoon on page 25. Explain that it was published widely in the colonies after it first appeared in Ben Franklin's *Pennsylvania Gazette* on May 9, 1754. Have students analyze the cartoon, using these questions: What did the publisher want the colonies to do? *(unite into a colonial nation)* What does the snake stand for? *(the colonies)*

Have partners brainstorm ideas for their own political cartoons. Their topics should be chosen from their study of U.S. history so far. For example, they might do a cartoon about relationships between Europeans and Native Americans, or about life in a colonial city. Have them draw their cartoons and display them on a bulletin board. SYNTHESIZING

Pitt Steps In

With the help of the colonists and their Native American allies, the British won the French and Indian War. But another conflict soon arose over who should pay for the war.

ASK

1. What was General Amherst's opinion of the colonists and the Native Americans? *(He didn't like the colonists and he detested the Native Americans.)*

2. Who was William Pitt, and how was he involved in the war? *(He was the English foreign secretary, and so was in charge of the war. He sent more troops to North America and gave Amherst instructions on how to beat the French.)*

3. How did Amherst carry out Pitt's orders? *(He laid siege to and took Louisbourg, gaining control of the St. Lawrence. He had Warraghiyagey and the Iroquois take control of the Niagara River. General Wolfe then took Quebec, and Amherst and Warraghiyagey took Montreal.)*

Ponder
Why did it take diplomats three years to work out the Treaty of Paris?

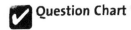 **Question Chart**

DISCUSS

1. Why was control of the St. Lawrence and Niagara rivers so important to the outcome of the war? *(The French used these rivers to supply their troops. If the English could gain control of them, they could cut off the French troops from supplies coming from France. That would make it easier for the English to win.)*

2. Refer students to the caption of the map on page 33. Ask: How did the French and Indian War solve one conflict for the British while introducing another? *(The British gained control of disputed North American lands, but decided the colonies should help pay the huge cost. That would provoke conflict between England and the colonies.)*

WRITE

Have students write a paragraph giving a possible explanation for the increase in British government spending during the French and Indian War. Students should include costs of sending troops, costs of ships and supplies, and so on.

LITERACY LINKS

Words to Discuss

foreign secretary
diplomats
siege

Discuss: Which two terms describe persons who serve their country? *(foreign secretary, diplomats)* What are some things that happen when a fortress is under siege? *(bombardment, supplies cut off, starvation)*

Reading Skills
Evaluating Visual Aids

Direct students to the painting *Death of General Wolfe* on page 32 and explain that it was completed in 1771, 12 years after the battle. The painter was Benjamin West, a renowned American artist, who was at the time of the battle only 19 years old and living in Philadelphia. Have students discuss how true-to-life they think this scene might be. Remind them that there were no photographers at the time. ANALYZING

Skills Connection
Geography

Have students use the Resource map on pages 214-215 to identify the natural resources the English gained control of after the war. *(fur, forests, waterways)* Then refer students to the map on page 33. Ask students to write a proposal describing how the colonists might use these resources.

Au Revoir (Goodbye), France

After the war, lands controlled by the French went to Great Britain. For their support, the Iroquois get nothing. Worse yet, land-hungry colonists began looking to occupy the Indian lands.

ASK

1. What is the meaning of the chapter title? (Au revoir *means "good-bye"; the author is referring to the fact that after the French and Indian War, France lost its North American colonies.*)

2. How did the Treaty of Paris change European land claims in North America? *(With the exception of two small islands, France gave up all its land. All land from the Atlantic to the Mississippi was claimed by Great Britain. New Orleans and the land west of the Mississippi were claimed by Spain.)*

3. At the time, who was living on most of the lands west of the Mississippi? *(Native Americans)*

4. Who was Junipero Serra? *(He was a Catholic priest who built missions in California.)*

 Ponder
Could the relations between colonists and Native Americans have been better? How?

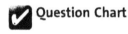 **Question Chart**

DISCUSS

1. What was the situation of the Native Americans after the war? *(The English no longer needed them as allies. They lost their French trading partners. Their lives were threatened by disease, and their lands continued to be taken away.)*

2. Have students complete Resource 2 (TG page 76) to show territorial claims in North America by European countries. Have them complete Resource 3 (TG page 77) to work with a primary source document.

3. Ask students who they think were the big winners and big losers of the war. *(England won huge territories, although the war costs balanced that. The colonists no longer had to deal with Indian attacks or French threats, and could settle new land. The French lost their colonies, and the Indians lost their French trading partners and their land.)*

WRITE

Ask students to imagine themselves living in the English colonies after the war. Have them write a dialogue among a Native American, a colonist, a British official, and a Spaniard about what should be done with the lands west of the Appalachians.

L I T E R A C Y   L I N K S

Words to Discuss

mission
presidio

Have students provide definitions for the words from the context on page 35. Ask: What was the purpose of a mission? *(to provide living quarters for Spanish settlers)* a presidio? *(to protect the missions)*

Reading Skills
Comparing and Contrasting

Have students complete a two-column chart on the chalkboard contrasting the attitudes toward Native Americans of Sir Jeffrey Amherst and Sir William Johnson. Be sure they include details supporting their ideas. Have students draw a conclusion about why these men had such different attitudes. INFERRING

Skills Connection
Language

Have interested students research the Cajun language—the mixture of French, English, Spanish, and African dialects spoken by some of the descendants of Acadians in Louisiana. Ask them to present a word list to the class.

THINKING ABOUT THE THEMES

The following questions will help students relate the book's themes to the content of Part 1. You may wish to use the questions for classroom discussion or have students answer them in written form.

1. What changes in the colonies were brought about by the French and Indian War? *(The French were driven from North America, and British control over the colonies grew stronger.)*

2. How did the results of Peter Zenger's trial advance the cause of freedom in the colonies? *(It gave the colonists freedom of the press, freedom of speech, and trial by jury.)*

3. Draw students' attention to the other themes that you posted around the room. Give them the opportunity to explore the relevance of these themes to Part 1. Accept choices that are supported by sound reasoning.

4. Draw students' attention to the themes that have been posted around the room. Give them the opportunity to explore the relevance of these themes to Part 1. Accept choices that are supported by sound reasoning.

ASSESSING PART 1

Use Check-Up 1 (TG page 68) to assess student learning.

NOTE FROM JOY HAKIM

To get a sense of the chronology of history, a timeline strung across the classroom—with clothespins holding key dates, events, pictures of people—is very helpful. What we want is for children to have a sense of sequence of the journey through time. But for most children, memorized dates have little meaning. A sophisticated sense of time comes gradually. As far as expecting children to remember dates, I believe only a few key years are essential.

PROJECTS AND ACTIVITIES

▶ Colonial Reporters

Assign students to write news stories about the Zenger trial. The stories should have headlines and should answer as many of the "five W's" of reporting *(Who? What? Where? When? Why?)* as possible. Students who wish to read the full transcript of the trial can locate it at **http://personal.pitnet.net/primarysources/zenger.html.**

▶ Colonial Songwriters

Have students write lyrics for a song about Warraghiyagey—his dual identity and his accomplishments as a colonial and military leader. They may wish to set their lyrics to a favorite song.

▶ Colonial Mapmakers

Have students work in small groups to create a large version of the map on page 33. If possible, provide an opaque projector or allow students to trace a photocopied enlargement of the map. Then assign groups to make spot art for each of the battles shown. Encourage students to use encyclopedias or other reference books to gather information about uniforms and geographic locations. Remind students that pictures in the textbook are also good sources of details.

▶ Timeline

Have students check their timeline against the one shown on page 33. Remind them that the timeline on this page shows only the events of the French and Indian War. Students' timeline should also include the Zenger trial (1735), the War of Jenkins' Ear (1738-1747), and Oglethorpe's victory at St. Augustine (1740).

★★ **FACTS TO SHARE** ★★

Between 1740 and 1760, the population of the English colonies increased dramatically, with some colonies doubling in size. The population of South Carolina, for example, increased from 45,000 to 94,070. This growth was due to births among whites and enslaved Africans as well as continuing immigration and importation of slaves.

Blazing New Trails

During the French and Indian War, Andrew Burnaby, an English clergyman, toured the colonies. In 1760, he wrote: "Nothing can exceed the jealousy . . . which they possess in regard for each other. . . . [W]ere they left to themselves, there would soon be a civil war from one end of the continent to the other. . . ." Burnaby failed to see that common ideals and beliefs tied the colonies together or that these ideals would change bickering colonists into American patriots. Part 2 describes the spirit of independence that helped fuel conflict with England.

SETTING GOALS

The goals for students in Part 2 are to:
• explain why the colonists moved toward independence.
• understand "American" character traits.
• recognize the effects of expanding colonial settlement on Native Americans.
• list the rights of Englishmen that colonists would demand.

GETTING INTERESTED

Ask students to scan the chapter titles and illustrations of Chapters 7-10. Write the Part title—*Blazing New Trails*—on the chalkboard. Ask students what this expression means. Ask: What "trails" are being blazed in modern times? *(space exploration, electronics, medicine, entertainment)* If you were a colonist in the 1760s, what trails might you be blazing? *(moving westward, seeking independence, learning how to live in a new land)*

Working with Timelines
Tell students that their timelines are going to become very crowded. They may want to choose a symbol such as a firecracker to indicate milestones on the road to independence

Using Maps
Refer students to the map on page 37. Discuss: How did the map of North America change as a result of the French and Indian War? *(France no longer controlled any territory. The land was divided between Spain and England.)*

Staying in Charge

England tried to control the westward movement of colonists with the Proclamation of 1763. But independent-minded pioneers like Daniel Boone had no intention of following orders from far-off England.

ASK

1. What country wanted to stay in charge? *(England)* What did it want to stay in charge of? *(its American colonies)* Why would that be difficult? *(Great Britain was far away from the colonies; colonists, Indians, and British officials are in conflict within the colonies.)*

2. What was the Proclamation of 1763? *(proclamation prohibiting the colonists from settling west of the Appalachians, leaving the lands to the Indians)*

3. Why did the colonists ignore the Proclamation of 1763? *(They wanted to move westward; they wanted more land.)*

4. What did the westward movement mean for the Indians? *(As more settlers came, the Indians lost their land. Their way of life was being destroyed.)*

Ponder
What conclusions can you draw about the kinds of people living in the colonies—and the potential conflicts among them?

✔ Question Chart

DISCUSS

1. What seeds of conflict were sewn west of the Appalachians? *(conflict over land between settlers and Native Americans; conflict over control between settlers and the faraway English government)*

2. Look at the map on page 37. Using what you know about the colonists and the size of the western territory, explain why it was almost impossible for the English to enforce the Proclamation of 1763. *(Too many colonists wanted western land, and the territory was too big for the English to enforce the proclamation.)*

WRITE

Ask students to imagine themselves as colonists moving westward. Have them write a diary entry describing a typical day in the wilderness.

L I T E R A C Y   L I N K S

Words to Discuss

    Great Awakening
    proclamation
    speculator

Refer students to the Wake Up! feature on page 36 for a description of the Great Awakening. Have them use a dictionary to find out which word comes from a Latin word meaning "to cry out" *(proclamation)* and which comes from a Latin word meaning "to see" *(speculator)*. Ask: Why would the Proclamation of 1763 anger land speculators?

Reading Skills
Identifying Cause and Effect

Ask students to describe the cause-effect chain resulting from the French and Indian War. Students might make a cause-effect diagram: *Cause:* Great Britain wins French and Indian War; *Effect:* Colonists and Indians fight over land; *Effect:* Britain issues Proclamation of 1763; *Effect:* Colonists ignore proclamation and begin taking Indian lands. ANALYZING

Skills Connection
Geography

Refer students to the map on page 37 and have them identify the two major western rivers. *(Ohio, Mississippi)* Ask students why such waterways were important to pioneers. *(transportation, rich farmland)* Have students locate the Appalachian Mountains and explain why finding gaps through these mountains was important. *(The steep mountains blocked westward movement; gaps were the only places pioneers could get their wagons through.)*

What Is an American?

Even before the Revolution, Hector St. John Crevecoeur sensed the creation of a new people called "Americans." Their society was a unique blend of English liberty and a sense of freedom and opportunity spawned by a vast frontier.

ASK

1. Name some things that Hector St. John Crevecoeur said made America special. *(absence of aristocrats, opportunity to have a farm, acting on new principles, mixing of peoples, freedom to think and believe what you want)*

2. What was Crevecoeur's warning to the Old World? *(that the "new race of men . . . will one day cause great change in the world")*

3. What happened while Crevecoeur was in Europe? *(Indians attacked his home, burning his house, killing his wife, and kidnapping two of his children.)*

4. What did Crevecoeur think of America after this tragedy? *(He kept his faith in America.)*

 Ponder
If Crevecoeur could visit your classroom, how would you answer his question, *What is an American?*

✔️ **Question Chart**

DISCUSS

1. Besides England, where did colonial settlers come from? *(Have students use their previous reading to identify the Netherlands, Scotland, Germany, Africa, Sweden, and France.)* How might living with people from different backgrounds create a new culture? *(Possible response: People combine customs and ideas from many places.)*

2. Have students use Resource 4 (TG page 78) to graph the population of the English colonies.

3. Remind students that slavery and restrictions on religious practice existed in the colonies. Discuss whether these things meant that Crevecoeur was wrong to be so impressed with America and the "new race of men."

WRITE

Ask students to write a book review of *Letters of an American Farmer* for a colonial newspaper. Encourage students to use what they've learned about groups living in the colonies to form opinions about the validity of Crevecoeur's statements.

LITERACY LINKS

Words to Discuss

yeoman farmers
posterity

Have students use the context on page 39 to define *yeoman farmers*. Have them use the last quote from Crevecoeur on page 40 to determine the meaning of *posterity*. Ask: What is a synonym for *posterity*? *(descendants)*

Reading Skills
Analyzing Text Features

Call attention to the way the text on page 40 is organized: the author introduces the main points in regular type, followed by Crevecoeur's words in italic type. Discuss: Why did the author use this kind of organization? How effective is it? *(The author describes Crevecoeur's most important ideas, then uses his own words to support the ideas. The difference in type makes the organization clear.)*
ANALYZING

Skills Connection
Science

Call attention to the American Pie feature on page 40. Ask: Why would the colonists go to such trouble to dry fruit? *(They didn't have refrigerators. Drying preserved the fruit so there would be apples year-round.)* Ask volunteers to research how drying preserves food and what kinds of foods are often dried today. Encourage students to report their findings to the class.

A Girl Who Always Did Her Best

Eliza Lucas's life is an example of how colonial experience changed the world. In an era when women had few rights, Eliza carved out a role as a scientist and business manager.

ASK

1. Describe the two social worlds in the colonies. *(Frontier: mostly classless, people were judged by what they could do. Structured colonies: society of rank and class. Both produced independent-minded people.)* To which world did Eliza Lucas belong? *(The structured colonies; she was the daughter of privileged plantation owners.)*

2. What did Lucas do before she married Charles Pinckney? *(ran her family's plantations and household, experimented with cash crops, studied law)*

3. Why can Lucas be called a Founding Mother? *(She was intelligent and independent-minded. She raised children who would play important roles in the future of America.)*

4. Have students complete Resource 5 (TG page 79) to compare and contrast primary and secondary sources about the life of colonial slaves.

Ponder
Think about the positive images of hard workers we have in our popular culture. Do you think Americans work too hard? Why or why not?

DISCUSS

1. Why was learning a wide range of skills important to colonists? *(Many had to grow their food, sew their clothing, build their houses, and so on.)*

2. Would you say that Eliza Lucas Pinckney was the kind of person who would want to be ruled by the British government? Why or why not? *(No. She thought for herself, took care of herself, and felt her future was in her own hands.)*

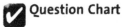 **Question Chart**

WRITE

Have students design a Founding Mother award for Lucas. The award should honor her accomplishments and spirit of independence. Students should create a form for the award (such as a medallion or plaque) and prepare an accompanying citation that gives reasons for selecting Lucas for the honor.

LITERACY LINKS

Words to Discuss

indigo
Founding Mother

Point out that *found*, the root of the word *founding*, has multiple meanings. Challenge students to use a dictionary to list different meanings of *found*, and to tell which of these meanings applies to *Founding Mother*.

Meeting Individual Needs
Visual Learners

To help students understand the description of colonial class structure on page 42, draw on the board a large triangle divided into six horizontal sections. Have a volunteer fill in the types of people in each class, with help from the rest of the class.

Skills Connection
Science

Eliza Pinckney experimented with producing silk. Since then, many attempts have been made to establish silk production in the United States, but with little success. Ask volunteers to research how silk is produced and why it has failed here. Have researchers present their findings to the class. Students might visit *www.insects.org/ced1/seric.html* for information.

The Rights of Englishmen

English barons struck a blow for freedom in 1215 by forcing King John to sign an agreement that granted the barons certain rights. Over the centuries, these rights were expanded, giving English citizens more freedom.

ASK

1. What did the English nobles want from King John? *(basic rights)*
2. Why was the Magna Carta important? *(It began a shift of power away from rulers and toward people who are governed.)*
3. What is the right of *habeas corpus*? *(A person can't be arrested and held for no reason.)*
4. What happened in the Glorious Revolution? *(Parliament, representing the English people, gave more power to the English people than to the English monarchs.)*

◉ Ponder
Remind students of the Zenger trial from Chapter 1. Why do people go to jail and risk their lives in order to win basic rights?

✔ Question Chart

DISCUSS

1. Why did the English nobles believe that they needed protection against their monarch? *(Their monarch had the power of life and death over them. King John abused the power so terribly that the barons rose against him.)*
2. What rights that we have now were first guaranteed by the Magna Carta? *(trial by jury*, habeas corpus, *no self-incrimination)* How did writing these down protect the people from evil government actions? *(It meant that the monarch—or the government—no longer had absolute power over the people.)*

WRITE

Have students describe the nobles' grievances, then have them write a "mini carta" that describes the rights the nobles wanted. Finally, invite students to role-play the nobles' rebellion.

LITERACY LINKS

Words to Discuss

Magna Carta   *habeas corpus*
Glorious Revolution writ
Bill of Rights   constitution

Have students use a dictionary and context to determine the meaning of the words and phrases. Ask: How does *habeas corpus* protect people? Under what circumstances would people want to create a *constitution*? What meaning do the words *bill* and *writ* have in common?

Reading Skills
Analyzing Perspective

Have partners find words the author uses to describe the Magna Carta and the Glorious Revolution. *(one of the world's greatest documents of freedom; an important right; something revolutionary; especially glorious)* Then have students write a sentence or two explaining how the author's choice of words reveals her opinion of these topics. SYNTHESIZING

THINKING ABOUT THE THEMES

The following questions will help students relate the book's themes to the content of Part 2. You may wish to use the questions for classroom discussion or have students answer them in written form.

1. In the 1760s the colonies were in a dither. They wanted to be part of England, but they also wanted more rights and independence. What were some reasons they wanted to remain loyal to England? What were some reasons they wanted independence? *(Loyal: England had protected them in the war against France, many people had friends and family in England. Independence: England wanted the colonies to pay for the French and Indian War; England was far away.)*

2. Hector St. John Crevecoeur said "There is room for everybody in America." Based on what you've read, was that true? Explain. *(Yes, people from many nations settled in America; No, the colonists were taking land from the Indians, who were not wanted; African-Americans were enslaved.)*

3. What were some of the conditions in the American colonies that helped create a spirit of independence? *(The colonies were far away from England; the colonists wanted to move westward to settle or make money; frontier settlers made their own laws; colonists created a new life.)*

4. Draw students' attention to the themes that have been posted around the room. Give them the opportunity to explore the relevance of these themes to Part 2. Accept choices that are supported by sound reasoning.

ASSESSING PART 2

Use Check-Up 2 (TG page 69) to assess student learning.

NOTE FROM JOY HAKIM

I try to give my readers facts and ideas and let them argue about them. And after they get into the material they seem to do just that. The most passionate discussions we have are often about politics. Well, history is just the politics of the past.

PROJECTS AND ACTIVITIES

▶ Moving Westward

Have students individually or in small groups write a fictional account of one family choosing to head west beyond the Appalachians in 1763. Stories should include reasons for moving, opinions of the Proclamation of 1763, and the route followed. Allow time for students to read their stories aloud.

▶ Make 'em Laugh

Refer students to the cartoon on page 38 and guide them in identifying some of the ways in which the cartoon pokes fun at Franklin. *(Franklin is holding a piece of paper—perhaps the Proclamation of 1763—to prevent the colonists from moving westward and taking Indian lands, but the colonists ignore him; a strange animal appears between his legs)* Have students create their own cartoon criticizing the colonists for their unfair treatment of the Indians. Students might also create a cartoon about Dr. Johnson or King John.

▶ Speak Up!

Have students review the rights of English citizens in the 1760s. Then ask students to work in teams to prepare a short oral statement in which a colonist expresses his or her understanding of the rights granted to citizens under English law. Each speech should begin with the following words: "My name is _____. As an English citizen I believe I am entitled to certain rights and liberties. My rights include _____."

★★ FACTS TO SHARE ★★

Did you know that the blue in blue jeans comes from indigo? Although in modern times the dye is synthesized chemically, about 14,000 tons of indigo are produced each year. The dye has long been important in clothing. Some ancient Egyptian mummies were wrapped in cloth died with indigo. During the American Revolution, indigo was so valuable that it was used as currency when paper money lost its value.

The Sparks of War

Stiff-backed British policies brought changes in the thinking of even moderate colonial leaders such as Pennsylvania's John Dickinson. "Heaven itself hath made us free," thundered Dickinson in 1768. Part 3 traces the events that provoked one of the most radical forms of political conflict—revolution.

SETTING GOALS

The goals for students in Part 3 are to:
- describe the causes underlying the American Revolution.
- identify and describe the roles of major Revolutionary figures.
- contrast the goals of the British and the Americans.
- describe the opening salvos of the American Revolution.

GETTING INTERESTED

1. Encourage students to discuss what can happen in life when conflicts between people grow more frequent and more intense. *(Possible outcomes: rifts between people, fights, divorce, all-out war)* Which seems to be the most likely outcome of the British-American conflict? *(war)*

2. Elicit from students taxes that Americans pay to the government (income taxes, property taxes, taxes on gasoline, and so on). Then ask: Suppose the government could just place new taxes on people without their approval, and they had to pay or be thrown in jail. What kind of conflict might that create? *(People would probably protest, refuse to pay the taxes, go to jail or fight until the government changed the law.)*

Working with Timelines

If you have created a class timeline, explain that the decade students will be reading about in this Part—1765-1775—will be full of events important to the history of the United States. Elicit ideas of how to display these events on the timeline without making it too crowded (for instance, symbols for events, mini-timelines attached to the main timeline).

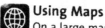

Using Maps

On a large map of the 13 colonies, have students locate the major cities of colonial America. Ask volunteers to use a map scale to figure out the distance between any two cities. Point out that some colonists thought it was easier to go from Boston to London than from Boston to Williamsburg. Discuss: How was travel on land different in colonial America than it is today?

A Taxing King

The British tried to raise revenues by taxing stamps and tea. Instead of paying, the colonists sent this message: "No taxation without representation." If the British would not allow them to be represented in Parliament, they would not pay British taxes.

ASK

1. What made the colonists mad at the British king and his ministers? *(The king and his ministers did not respect the colonists; they asked the colonists to pay unfair taxes.)*
2. What did the colonists insist on having? *(the right to vote on their own taxes, just as English people did, through representatives in Parliament)*
3. Why was the Stamp Act repealed, or ended? *(The colonists refused to pay it.)*
4. How did the colonists rebel against the tax on tea? *(They dumped chests of tea in the Boston Harbor.)*

Ponder
What do you think the Indians thought about the colonists disguising themselves as Indians for the Boston Tea Party?

Question Chart

DISCUSS

1. How did the British actions against the American colonists backfire? *(Rather than forcing the Americans to accept the taxes, these actions heightened American feeling against the British and united colonists in their opposition.)*
2. **Sourcebook:** Read items I-VII of the Resolutions of the Stamp Act Congress *(Sourcebook, #10)*. What are the colonists saying they want? *(the same rights as other English subjects; the right to not be taxed without being represented in Parliament)*
3. What did John Rutledge mean when he said that England should "go to school with the Iroquois"? *(He admired the way each of the six Iroquois nations were self-governing but worked together when necessary, such as in times of war.)*

WRITE

Ask students to write a persuasive letter that John Rutledge might have sent to a South Carolina newspaper, with the headline *Lessons We Should Learn from the Haudenosaunee.*

L I T E R A C Y   L I N K S

Words to Discuss

Stamp Act   repeal

Point out that *act* is a multiple-meaning word. Direct students to use context clues and a dictionary to determine the meaning used in this chapter. Ask: What is a synonym for *repeal*? *(end, abolish)*

Reading Skills
Analyzing Point of View

Refer students to the No Right to Tax feature on page 50. Ask: What does Pitt think Britain should do? *(not tax the Americans)* Does Pitt's argument seem emotional or logical? *(logical)* What makes you think so? *(He talks about how the colonial assemblies have always collected their own taxes; he says England has never taxed the colonies without their consent.)* ANALYZING

Analyzing Cartoons

Direct students to the cartoon on page 53 and ask them to notice elements that make the cartoon funny. Discuss how the cartoon uses irony and exaggeration to make its point—having a funeral for a stamp; having people behave in a way that is highly unlikely. ANALYZING

The Firebrands

The actions and words of three firebrands helped spark the war. From north to south, people soon knew the names of Samuel Adams, Thomas Paine, and Patrick Henry.

ASK

1. The firebrands are from different backgrounds. How are all three alike? *(They all have the ability to stir people's minds and hearts.)*
2. Why is travel between colonies very difficult? *(poor roads)*
3. Why was Sam Adams wanted by the British? *(He tried to unite the colonies against England.)*
4. How did Patrick Henry stir up the Virginia House of Burgesses? *(He cried out for liberty.)*
5. What effect did Tom Paine's *Common Sense* have on many colonists? *(It changed their attitudes toward England.)*

 Ponder
How could you use your ability to speak and write to persuade others to join a cause you believe in strongly?

 **Question Chart**

DISCUSS

1. How did the firebrands help to move the American colonies toward revolution? *(They stirred up the colonists' emotions and persuaded them to rebel.)* Why was it difficult to unite the colonies against the British? *(The colonists didn't think of themselves as part of one country. Because travel was difficult, the colonists didn't communicate with each other and didn't know each other.)*
2. What special talents did Adams, Paine, and Henry have? *(Adams: busybody, organizer, great thinker and writer; Paine: great writer; Henry: great speaker)* How was their message spread across the colonies? *(Adams started the committees of correspondence; Paine published books; Henry spoke in the Virginia House of Burgesses.)*
3. Have students use Resource 6 (TG page 80) to compare the Firebrands.

WRITE

Ask students to imagine that they are colonial firebrands. Have them write a broadside, or a one-sheet poster, calling for action against the British and why it should be taken.

LITERACY LINKS

Words to Discuss

firebrand   deist
committee of correspondence

Have students use the chapter context to answer these questions: Which firebrand was a deist? *(Tom Paine)* If you were a firebrand, how would you use the committee of correspondence? *(to communicate with other firebrands)*

Skills Connection
Geography

Distribute copies of Resource 7 (TG page 81) to give students further information about the road system in the colonies.

Public Speaking

Invite students with an interest in public speaking or acting to imagine that they are colonial firebrands. Ask them to develop short, fiery speeches to persuade their listeners to take action to free themselves from British rule. Suggest that students use appropriate phrasing, intonation, and gestures in delivering their speeches to the class.

A Massacre in Boston

Hostility between British soldiers and colonists led to rabble-rousing and then to the death of some colonists—further stirring revolutionary sentiment in the colonies.

ASK

1. What were the causes of the Boston Massacre? *(The Quartering Act required colonists to house British soldiers. This caused tension between soldiers and Bostonians. A mob of colonists confronted some soldiers, taunting them and throwing things at them until the soldiers fired into the mob.)*

2. What effect did Paul Revere's engraving of the Boston Massacre have? *(It fired up the colonists against the British.)*

3. What were the results of the First Continental Congress? *(The Congress advised colonists to form militias and stop buying British goods, passed 10 resolutions about the rights of the colonists, talked about common problems, sent a petition to King George, agreed to meet again if things got worse.)*

DISCUSS

1. Discuss the nature of conflict and the way it can build—(1) differing views, (2) bad feelings, (3) angry words and threats, and (4) violence. Encourage students to recall events in the conflict between British and Americans matching these steps. *(1. Quartering Act announced; 2. soldiers arrive; 3. colonists taunt soldiers; 4. soldiers fire on colonists)*

2. What was John Adams fighting for? How does this relate to his defense of the British soldiers after the Boston Massacre? *(Adams was fighting for the chance to form a government based on fair play and self-government. Giving the soldiers a fair trial, despite public opinion, was basic to that kind of government.)*

WRITE

Invite students in groups of four to conduct an interview with John and Sam Adams about the Boston Massacre and Continental Congress. One student serves as interviewer, two others role play the Adamses, a fourth serves as recorder. Have all four students review the transcript.

 Ponder
How did the trial of the British soldiers and the meeting of the Continental Congress show the spirit of democracy and freedom that was developing in America?

 **Question Chart**

L I T E R A C Y   L I N K S

Words to Discuss

| Quartering Act | militia |
| propaganda | deserters |

Elicit from students the meanings of *quarter* as a verb and a noun, and to tell which meaning applies in the chapter. Have them find the meaning of *propaganda* in a dictionary. Point out that, although the word often has a negative connotation, it actually denotes something that is neither good nor bad.

Reading Skills
Analyzing Primary Sources

Have students look at the illustration on page 65 and read the caption. Ask: Why would this engraving have made the colonists mad? *(It looks as if the unarmed colonists are being murdered by the British soldiers.)* Emphasize that there was no photography or video and an illustration had great power—especially one that was from an "eyewitness." CONNECTING

Meeting Individual Needs
Visual Learners

Encourage students to create their own illustration of the Boston Massacre. They might aim to produce either a more realistic picture than Revere's or one that can be used as propaganda against the British, as Revere's was.

One If by Land, Two If by Sea

Conflict turned into war when minutemen and redcoats scuffled at Lexington and Concord, setting the American colonists solidly on the road toward becoming a new nation.

ASK

1. Why did Paul Revere and William Dawes ride out from Boston on the night of April 18, 1775? *(They had learned that the British were going to march on Concord the next morning to capture the Patriots' gunpowder as well as Sam Adams and John Hancock. They rode out to alert the minutemen to prepare for the attack.)*

 Ponder
Why did Emerson call the shooting at Lexington and Concord "the shot heard round the world"?

2. Have volunteers read the Who Started It? feature aloud. Ask: Based on these descriptions, what sort of fighting occurred at Lexington? *(The battle was short and the British overwhelmed the Americans, who retreated in confusion.)*

3. How was the fighting at Concord different than at Lexington? *(The Americans returned the British fire, and it was the redcoats' turn to retreat and to be chased by the Americans.)*

 **Question Chart**

DISCUSS

1. How do you think the battles of Lexington and Concord affected the colonists? *(They were probably surprised and gleeful that they had defeated the British; they might have felt more confident that they could win a war against the British.)* Do you think all the colonists were pleased? *(No, the Loyalists were probably very unhappy.)*

2. Look at the engraving and caption on page 75. What conclusions can you draw about relationships between Patriots and Loyalists after Lexington and Concord? *(The two sides became even more divided, and violence between them flared.)*

WRITE

Ask students to write a paragraph explaining whether they think the revolution will be a people's war. Their paragraph should contrast the minutemen and the redcoats and identify leaders on both sides.

L I T E R A C Y   L I N K S

Words to Discuss

Patriot minutemen
Loyalist

Ask students to think of other words related to *Patriot (patriotic, patriotism)*, then have them use a dictionary to find the Latin root of the word and its meaning *(pater, "father")*.

Reading Skills
Asking Questions

Guide students in creating questions based on the text and the illustrations in this chapter. Questions might relate to how the revolutionary volunteers became organized to oppose the British; how reports of the battles reached England; and what happened to Revere after he was arrested. Questions might be used as the basis for independent research.
QUESTIONING

Skills Connection
Geography

Have small groups use the maps on pages 68 and 70-71 to describe the landforms in the Boston harbor. (They should note the peninsulas and islands.) Then have students describe the routes taken by Revere, Dawes, and Prescott. You might suggest that students present their descriptions in the form of a dialogue in which the three riders tell each other about their journeys.

An American Original

The British possessed a large professional army, but the colonists boasted the raw courage of backwoods fighters such as Ethan Allen, who proved his daring by capturing Fort Ticonderoga.

ASK

1. Before the Revolution, who were Ethan Allen and the Green Mountain Boys fighting? *(New Yorkers who wanted Allen and other Vermont farmers to pay them for the land or leave.)*

2. How did Ethan Allen help the Patriot war effort? *(He and his men captured the British Fort Ticonderoga on Lake Champlain. He led an American force into Canada to try to capture Montreal.)*

3. How were Ethan Allen and Benedict Arnold different? *(Arnold was a "proper soldier," dressed in a fancy uniform; Allen was wild and rough. Arnold became a traitor; Allen was loyal to the colonists.)*

 **Ponder**
What makes a person an "original"? What Americans, past or present, might be put in this category?

☑ **Question Chart**

DISCUSS

1. Contrast Allen's physical appearance and manner with his behavior toward his enemies. *(Although he was big, powerful, and crude in manner, he was not a killer. He took Fort Ticonderoga without casualties; he never shot "Yorkers" or Redcoats.)*

2. Reread the feature on page 79. Call volunteers to the board to list the ideas from the Enlightenment that were important in making Americans seek self-government. *(think for yourself; people have natural rights; government should be run for the people, not the rulers)*

WRITE

Ask students to write a ballad or poem about Ethan Allan that portrays his character and key events described in this chapter. Encourage students to set their words to music—to something old or to something original.

LITERACY LINKS

Words to Discuss

Green Mountain Boys
Enlightenment

Help students break the word *Enlightenment* into syllables. Point out the base word *light*. Explain that the other parts of the word are *affixes*—word parts added to a word to change its meaning or use in a sentence. Have students identify the prefix and suffixes in the word.

Reading Skills
Identifying Details

Ask students to identify details the author provides that help readers visualize Ethan Allen's appearance and manner. *(His language was rough and rowdy; He was a sinewy giant; famous for his strength; no one could tell Ethan Allen what to do; bluster, strong muscles, good mind; curser)*
VISUALIZING

Skills Connection
Geography

Have students use a topographical map of Vermont and New York to trace a route Allen might have taken from Bennington to Fort Ticonderoga. Encourage students to discuss why the fort was important and to identify the major city in Canada that is closest to the northern end of Lake Champlain. *(Montreal)*

THINKING ABOUT THE THEMES

The following questions will help students relate the book's themes to the content of Part 3. You may wish to use the questions for classroom discussion or have students answer them in written form.

1. Name three events that occurred between 1765 and 1776 and tell why they pushed the American colonists toward war against the British. (*Responses will vary, and may include Britain's efforts to tax the colonists and growing resistance to British authority; Britain's attempt to quarter soldiers in the colonies and seize colonial ammunition.*)

2. Compare the way the firebrands, the Continental Congress, and the minutemen and Green Mountain Boys contributed to revolution against Great Britain. (*Students should mention the firebrands' persuasive arguments, the Continental Congresses' list of rights and letter to King George, and the bravery of the soldiers in defeating the British armies.*)

3. Do you think Paul Revere's etching of the Boston Massacre is a work of propaganda? Why or why not? (*Answers will vary. Students should support their responses with logical reasoning and evidence.*)

4. Draw students' attention to the themes that have been posted around the room. Give them the opportunity to explore the relevance of these themes to Part 3. Accept choices that are supported by sound reasoning.

ASSESSING PART 1

Use Check-Up 3 (TG page 70) to assess student learning in Part 3.

NOTE FROM JOY HAKIM

One teacher who piloted my books had her class turn the chapters into dramatic presentations. Groups of students were each given a different chapter. I happened by for a visit and saw some wonderfully free and imaginative presentations.

PROJECTS AND ACTIVITIES

▶ Colonial Debate

Resolved That Thomas Paine is right: " 'tis time to part" from Great Britain. (To reflect a range of opinion, appoint some students to speak for the Loyalists. Others should speak for radical and moderate Patriots.)

▶ Colonial Autobiography

Assign students individually or in small groups to write a brief autobiographical statement for a figure they select from this Part. To get students started, write the following sentence frame on the chalkboard: My name is _____, and I am important in history because _____.

▶ Colonial Employers

Write the following incomplete advertisement on the chalkboard: WANTED: Firebrand to work with Sam Adams and other Patriots in Boston. Candidate for the job must be _____. Have students work in teams to complete the advertisement, focusing on the characteristics of firebrands mentioned in the text. Call on teams to read their ads aloud.

▶ Colonial Travelers

Have students pretend they are delegates from Richmond, Virginia headed to Philadelphia for the First Continental Congress. Have students refer to the feature on page 58 and write diary entries describing their method or route of travel.

▶ Colonial Editorials

Refer students to Who Started It? on page 70. Call on students to write a response to this question from either the Patriot or British point of view. Then challenge students to draw sketches that the *Salem Gazette* and the *London Gazette* might have run to illustrate each account of the battles. You might post these sketches on the bulletin board.

★★ **FACTS TO SHARE** ★★

When Allen's death seemed near, his doctor said to him, "General, I fear the angels are waiting for you." The crusty Allen replied, "Waiting, are they? Well—let 'em wait."

The Road to Independence

On June 7, 1776, Richard Henry Lee opened one of the great debates in our history, declaring in the Second Continental Congress: "Resolved: that these United Colonies are, and of right out to be, free and independent States. . . ." This resolution spurred the delegates to start thinking and talking about revolution waged in defense of "natural rights." The job of defining those rights fell to Thomas Jefferson. Part 4 covers the chain of events that led Americans to adopt a new language of freedom.

SETTING GOALS

The goals for students in Part 4 are to:
- identify the leaders of the Patriots.
- identify and describe the early battles of the American Revolution.
- explain the aims of the Declaration of Independence.
- explore the effects of the Declaration of Independence.

GETTING INTERESTED

1. On the chalkboard, draw a line representing the "road to independence." Ask volunteers to enter stops along the way that they have already investigated. *(refusing to obey the Proclamation of 1763; Boston Tea Party; firebrands' writings and speeches; Boston Massacre; Lexington and Concord, Fort Ticonderoga.)* Help the class to see that the road leads through many conflicts and will continue to do so.

2. Read aloud the selection from the Declaration of Independence on page 99. Guide students in identifying ideals expressed in this passage. *(equality, liberty, possession of unalienable rights, government by consent of the governed)* Ask why these ideals seemed extreme at the time. *(No other government had achieved them.)*

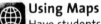 **Using Maps**
Have students locate Boston, Philadelphia, and Charleston on a classroom map. Discuss how small a part of the present United States this triangle represents, yet how important these cities were in the nation's history.

Reading Primary Sources
The primary sources Joy Hakim includes in this Part are written in a formal style that students rarely see in modern writing. You may wish to have small groups analyze particular pieces of writing to ensure understanding of these timeless documents.

On the Way to the Second Continental Congress

Few of the delegates who traveled to Philadelphia in 1775 wanted to rush headlong into revolution. However, with bullets flying in Boston, more wondered how long they could continue to call themselves English subjects.

ASK

Ponder
How were the delegates different from average colonists? How do you think such men will get along as they work together in the Congress?

Question Chart

1. Why are the Patriots and Loyalists arguing? *(Patriots want independence from Great Britain; Loyalists want to stay British subjects.)*
2. Who were some of the delegates to the Second Continental Congress? *(George Washington, John Adams, Sam Adams, Benjamin Franklin, Richard Henry Lee, Thomas Jefferson)*
3. The most popular delegates came from which colony? *(Virginia)*
4. What had Benjamin Franklin tried to do in Canada? *(get the Canadians to join the colonies in the revolution)*

DISCUSS

1. Men from the colonies are meeting to decide what to do about Great Britain. What qualities, skills, and achievements do you think these men should have? *(intelligence, courage, good sense, leadership, wide knowledge or education)* Invite students to name some of the men they have already met and describe their qualities, skills, and achievements.
2. Assign Resource 8 (TG page 82) to help students become more familiar with the delegates.
3. Which colonies sent more than one delegate? *(Virginia, Massachusetts, New Jersey, Pennsylvania)* How do you think the number of delegates for a colony was decided? *(based on population)* What does this tell you about the kind of government the colonists would want? *(one that fairly represented the people living in the colonies)*

WRITE

Although there was no television in 1775, ask students to prepare a list of questions for a TV interview of one of the delegates to the convention.

L I T E R A C Y   L I N K S

Words to Discuss

legislative authority
commonwealth

Ask students to read the A Virginian feature and identify the definition for *legislative authority (laws)*. Discuss: What is a legislature? Ask students to identify the two words that make up *commonwealth*. Discuss the two words in relation to the definition given on page 84.

Meeting Individual Needs
English Language Learners

Students may have difficulty pronouncing some of the proper names in this chapter. Have these students work with a native English speaker to practice pronouncing the names. You might also provide tape recordings of the names for students to hear and repeat.

Skills Connection
Geography/Math

Divide the class into small groups and assign each group one of the delegates. Have them identify his colony, find it on a map, and use the map scale to estimate the distance he traveled to Philadelphia. Students might also use the figures for stagecoach travel given on pages 57 and 59 to estimate how long the trip to Philadelphia would have taken.

Naming a General

The task of shaping ragged militia into a Continental army fell to George Washington. Rejection of the Olive Branch Petition by King George III helped ensure that Washington would remain on the battlefield for nearly six years.

ASK

1. Why did the colonists need a general? *(Someone had to organize the minutemen into an army.)*
2. What was dangerous about the job of General of the army? *(He was facing the most powerful enemy in the world—Great Britain.)*
3. How were John Adams and George Washington alike? *(They both did what they thought was best for the country.)*
4. Why were some people in England rooting for an American Revolution? *(They thought the American revolution would bring better government to England.)*

 Ponder

Suppose you were chosen as leader of the colonial army. What steps would you take to get the army ready for war? How would you inspire the army?

 **Question Chart**

DISCUSS

1. The year 1775 was a year of many conflicts within the colonies. What were some of those conflicts, and why did war seem unavoidable? *(Some Americans wanted to fight Britain, but others did not; colonial militia were ready to fight, but they were raggedy, not organized, and had no leader; Washington was chosen general, but he really did not want to be general; King George III refused the Olive Branch Petition.)*
2. What qualities and skills did George Washington have that made him a good choice for General of the army? *(skill as a military officer, talent, noble character, the ability to inspire others)*

WRITE

Refer students to the A Society of Patriotic Ladies feature on page 88. Invite students to create a poem about something they would give up or not do in order to protest against the British government.

LITERACY LINKS

Words to Discuss

Olive Branch Petition

Have students use a dictionary to find the meaning of *petition*. Help students understand that a petition is a formal plea or request that represents the wishes of a group of people. Discuss the symbolic meaning of an olive branch. Then ask students to infer what an Olive Branch Petition might request. *(peace)*

Reading Skills
Analyzing Rhetorical Devices

Have students reread the sidebar on page 88 and identify the author's play on words. *(body, meaning "anyone" and "legislative group")* Remind students that the author uses humor often in the book, and one of the devices she uses is words with multiple meanings. Have students find other words in the text that have more than one meaning. Then have them define the different meanings the word has and paraphrase the meaning the word has in the text. ANALYZING

The War of the Hills

The battle at Breed's Hill and Bunker Hill introduced the redcoats to Patriot sharpshooters. The British pushed the Patriots off the hills, but only at a terrible cost of life.

 Ponder

Breed's Hill and Bunker Hill are two small pieces of land. Do you think they were worth fighting for? Why or why not?

 **Question Chart**

ASK

1. How did the Massachusetts soldiers surprise the British at Breed's Hill? *(Overnight they built fortifications while the British slept.)*
2. Why might the Massachusetts soldiers have been scared of the British? *(The British were the best soldiers and had lots of weapons; the Americans were not trained to fight.)*
3. What weapons did the Revolutionary soldiers use? *(muskets with bayonets attached; rifles)*
4. Why did the Americans have to leave Breed's Hill and Bunker Hill? *(They ran out of gunpowder.)*

DISCUSS

1. Direct students to look at the illustrations on pages 90, 91, and 92. Discuss similarities and differences between these battles and the battles of Lexington and Concord. *(Differences: Lexington and Concord were fought in the countryside on flat ground; Bunker and Breed's were hills where the Americans built fortifications; the British used foot soldiers as well as gunboats; Americans won at Lexington and Concord; British won at the hills. Similarities: The British arrived by boat.)*
2. Who would you say won the battle of Breed's and Bunker hills? *(The British captured the hills and chased the Patriots away, but it cost them many more men than the Patriots lost. The Patriots proved they could stand their ground against the British army.)*

WRITE

Have students write an eyewitness account of the battles of Breed's and Bunker hills. Suggest that students use the format of either a news article or ballad.

LITERACY LINKS

Words to Discuss

fortifications   barracks
earthworks   bayonet

Direct students to use context on page 89 to determine the meaning of *fortifications. (trenches, barriers)* Ask: Which word names a kind of weapon? *(bayonet)* Have students use the chapter context on page 90 to figure out the meaning of *earthworks. (a barrier built by men from dirt and stone)*

Reading Skills
Questioning

Refer the class to The Little Drummer Boy feature on page 92. Prompt students to ask questions about the role of a drummer boy in the army. Suggest that students research information on this topic.
QUESTIONING

Skills Connection
Geography

Resource 9 (TG page 83) provides a graphic of the area involved in that conflict and asks students to use it and a text illustration to increase their understanding of the battle's logistics.

Fighting Palm Trees

When British ships attacked Fort Sullivan in Charleston Harbor in South Carolina, it seemed that even the trees fought back. Cannonballs stuck in the fort's soft palmetto wood, while Patriot cannons blasted the British ships.

ASK

1. How was William Pitt's idea about the American Revolution different from Lord North's? *(Pitt saw the Americans as just fighting for the same rights that English had gained; North thought the Americans should be taught a lesson.)*

2. How were the British surprised by the fort on Sullivan's Island? *(When they fired on it, the cannon balls stuck in the wooden siding.)*

3. Why couldn't the British soldiers get to Sullivan's Island? *(Their boats were stuck and the water was too deep for them to walk to the island.)*

 **Ponder**
Why is it important to think ahead, plan, and investigate before attacking an enemy?

✓ **Question Chart**

DISCUSS

1. Ask the class to review how geography worked for the Patriots and against the British at Breed's and Bunker hills. *(The Patriots were on the top, the British had to march upward against the Patriots' fire.)* Ask the class how geography worked again for the Patriots and against the British at Charleston. *(Logs made from the Palmetto trees caught the cannon balls fired by the British; the British ships got stuck on the sand bar in the harbor.)*

2. How do you think the British felt as they left Charleston Harbor after the battle? *(They must have been embarrassed, humiliated, and ashamed at their stupidity.)* What conclusions can you draw about the British, based on the mistakes they made at the battles of the hills and of Charleston? *(They are arrogant and underestimate the Americans.)*

WRITE

Ask students to write a paragraph describing the Charleston battle from either the American or British point of view. Call on volunteers to read their paragraphs aloud to contrast the points of view.

LITERACY LINKS

Words to Discuss

run aground
shoals

Discuss: The letter *a* is sometimes added as a prefix to a word, to add the meaning "in," "into," "on," or "at." Examples include *asleep, atop, apace.* What might *aground* mean? *(on ground)* Explain that when a ship runs aground, it comes to rest on soil or rocks and is unable to move. Have students use context clues on page 95 to determine the meaning of *shoals. (piece of rising ground; shallow water)*

Reading Skills
Comparing Texts

Encourage students to perform a choral reading of the poem on pages 96-97, breaking it into parts for different groups to read. Then ask students to compare and contrast the description in the poem with the description of the same events in the text on pages 95-96. Which is more interesting? Which has more details? Which is easier to read? CONNECTING

Skills Connection
Geography

Invite students to carefully examine the diagram of Fort Sullivan and the map of Sullivan's Island on page 97. Discuss: How is the fort positioned in relation to the harbor? *(It faces the harbor.)* Notice how the harbor narrows between the fort and the Lower Middle Ground. What made this a good place to build a fort? *(Ships sailing in the narrow part of the harbor would sail close to the fort and be better targets for the fort's cannons.)*

Declaring Independence

The Declaration of Independence introduced the world to the American interpretation of democracy. Its lofty principles of equality and liberty have guided generations of Americans.

ASK

1. What happened on July 4, 1776? *(Delegates to the Continental Congress approve the Declaration of Independence.)*

2. What were the three main things that Jefferson was supposed to state in the Declaration? *(tell what the Congress believed about good government; tell what King George had done wrong; announce that the colonies were free and independent states)*

3. What compromise did the delegates make about slavery? *(To get all the delegates to sign the Declaration, the mention of slavery was taken out.)*

4. How were Benjamin Banneker and Thomas Jefferson alike? How were they different? *(Alike: they both played the violin, they were both Enlightenment thinkers, they were both inventors and writers. Different: Banneker was African-American, Jefferson was white.)*

⊚ **Ponder**
Look at the picture of the draft of the Declaration of Independence on page 99. Why is it important that good ideas be put in writing and be well written?

✔ **Question Chart**

DISCUSS

1. How were some of the high ideals of the Declaration of Independence—such as "all men are created equal"—contradicted by society in America at the time? *(Slavery contradicted the Declaration's ideals, and many of the people who signed the Declaration were slave owners. Women were not allowed equal rights with men.)*

2. What do you think of the compromise the delegates made regarding the mention of slavery in the Declaration of Independence? *(Responses will vary.)*

WRITE

Ask students to write a letter to Arthur Middleton, delegate from South Carolina, whose picture appears on page 101. In their letter, students should express their opinion of the images portrayed in the picture and how those images relate to the ideals of the Declaration and to the realities of colonial life for most Americans.

LITERACY LINKS

Words to Discuss

declaration
consent of the governed
antislavery
compromise

Direct students to use a dictionary to find the Latin root of *declare*. *("to make clear")* Point out that the ending -*tion* can be added to a verb to change it to a noun, as in *converse/conversation*. Have students notice how the accented syllable shifts to the vowel before -*tion*. Ask: What does a written or spoken declaration do? *(clearly states what the writer wants)* Discuss the prefix *anti-*.

Reading Skills
Analyzing Rhetorical Devices

Refer the class to the feature on page 102. Ask: Which words does Banneker use to describe the bias that some colonists held against black people? *(the train of absurd and false ideas and opinions)* Paraphrase Banneker's beliefs about equality. *(Possible response: He believes that humans were created by the same god who gave them all the same senses and abilities, and that humans are all part of the same family, despite surface differences.)* ANALYZING

Analyzing Cartoons

Refer the class to the cartoon on page 100. Encourage them to brainstorm ideas for other actions that might symbolize a break—for example the breakup of a friendship, or a wild animal escaping from a cage. Invite students to apply one of these symbolic actions to a political or social situation and to illustrate it in a cartoon. Advise them that they should make clear who is who and what action is taking place. SYNTHESIZING

Signing Up

Today we call the delegates who signed the Declaration of Independence heroes. But King George III had another name for them—traitors.

ASK

1. What was difficult about signing the Declaration? *(The signers could be hung if Great Britain won the war.)*
2. Which delegate was most responsible for getting the others to sign the Declaration? *(John Adams)*
3. What did General Washington's troops do when they heard the Declaration? *(shouted hurrah and threw their hats into the air)*

Ponder
The delegates to the Continental Congress seemed willing to die for their beliefs. Do you think most Americans are as brave today? Why or why not?

 **Question Chart**

DISCUSS

1. When King George heard about the Declaration of Independence, he remarked gloomily, "If it succeeds, none need call it treason." What do you think he meant? *(The Declaration would be an act of treason only if the Patriots lost the war.)*
2. Fifty-six delegates signed the Declaration, but at least two did not—John Dickinson and Robert Livingston. What do you think it was like to be in a minority among the delegates at this time?

WRITE

Ask students to write an essay on the pros and cons of signing the Declaration of Independence.

LITERACY LINKS

Words to Discuss

forfeit	dissenting
gilded	pensive

Suggest that students use a dictionary to look up the meanings of the words. Ask: What is something you would not want to forfeit? What might be a dissenting opinion about fast foods? How would a gilded statue look? When might you have a pensive look?

Reading Skills
Understanding Literary Terms

Refer the class to An Awful Silence on page 105. Ask them to retell Colonel Harrison's joke. Explain that the literary term for this kind of joke is *gallows humor.* Help students understand that *gallows* refers to the frame used to hang people until they were dead, and then ask students why Harrison's joke is an example of gallows humor. *(It makes fun of a disastrous or life-threatening situation.)*
CONNECTING

Skills Connection
History/Art

Have students examine John Trumbull's painting on pages 104-105. Ask students how Trumbull conveys the solemnity of the occasion. *(The men all have solemn, thoughtful expressions on their faces.)* Explain that the painting took five years to complete because each figure is an exact likeness of the person, with one exception. Ask students to compare the painting with a photo of members of the current Congress.

THINKING ABOUT THE THEMES

The following questions will help students relate the book's themes to the content of Part 4. You may wish to use the questions for classroom discussion or have students answer them in written form.

1. Summarize the events of 1775-1776 that led up to the signing of the Declaration on July 4, 1776. *(The redcoats and minutemen had fought at Lexington and Concord; Patriots had taken the British fort at Ticonderoga; George III had refused to sign the Olive Branch Petition; redcoats and minutemen fought again at Breed's Hill, Bunker Hill, and Charleston.)*

2. Jefferson, Adams, and other delegates had conflicts over the issue of slavery. Still, slavery was not mentioned in the Declaration. Why? *(They thought that creating a Union was more important at that time than the issue of slavery.)*

3. How did John Hancock show that he was not a spoilsport? *(He was disappointed that he wasn't chosen commander of the Continental Army, but he supported Washington, and he was the first to sign the Declaration of Independence.)*

4. Draw students' attention to the themes that have been posted around the room. Give them the opportunity to explore the relevance of these themes to Part 4. Accept choices that are supported by sound reasoning.

ASSESSING PART 4

Use Check-Up 4 (TG page 71) to assess learning in Part 4.

NOTE FROM JOY HAKIM

Is anyone in your class a stamp collector? Who are some of the people on U.S. commemorative stamps? Assign a stamp to each student and have students write one or two paragraphs about the stamp that can be read aloud to the rest of the class.

PROJECTS AND ACTIVITIES

➤ Colonial Debate

Resolved: That the American Revolution could not be avoided. (To add interest to the debate, you might have some students take the parts of firebrands such as Thomas Paine and Patrick Henry, who felt war must come. Other students should speak for John Dickinson and Joseph Hewes, who felt there was room for freedom within the British Empire.)

➤ Colonial Poets

Read aloud the following lines written about Washington and the Continental army:

Huzzah, huzzah, to Washington and his band
With their brave help we'll have freedom in our land.

Then ask small groups of students to write and recite rhymes that identify or say something about various figures they have read about in Part 4.

➤ Colonial Biographer

Have students do additional research on Benjamin Banneker and prepare a report on this fascinating American.

➤ Colonial Cartoonist

Refer students to the political cartoon on page 88. Challenge students to draw a political cartoon of what became known as the Edenton Tea Party from the Patriot point of view. Post these cartoons on the bulletin board.

★★ **FACTS TO SHARE** ★★

When, in 1989, Chinese students poured into Tiananmen Square in China's capital of Beijing to demand political reform, they rallied support by reading aloud from the Declaration of Independence. They also carried signs bearing American slogans like *Give me liberty or give me death* and *Government of the people, by the people, and for the people*. Their final invocation of American ideals was their construction of a giant "Goddess of Democracy" statue in the square.

Fighting the War

In 1777, Lucy Knox wrote to her husband, General Henry Knox, "I hope that when you come home from war you will not consider yourself commander in chief of our house—but be convinced . . . that there is now such a thing as equal command." Her words reflected changes in America. The war effort involved men and women, young and old, whites and blacks. Part 5 tells the story of the "people's war" for independence.

SETTING GOALS

The goals for students in Part 5 are to:
- identify groups and individuals involved in the Revolution.
- describe the Patriots' major setbacks and triumphs.
- explain the turning points of the war.

GETTING INTERESTED

1. You might write this proverb from *Poor Richard's Almanack* on the board: "Little strokes fell great oaks." Ask: Why might this be good advice for the Patriots? Hang a sheet of poster board entitled *Little Strokes That Won the War*. As students read, have them enter examples of the Patriots' little strokes.

2. Although the Americans had had some successes, the war was just getting started. The British had the most feared army and most powerful navy on earth. Have students make predictions about what the Americans would have to do, what the British might do, and who might help the Americans. Students can list their predictions in their notebooks and check them as they read.

 Working with Timelines
Explain that all the events in this Part took place in a two-year period. Ask: How can these events be shown on the class timeline? Discuss how to link a micro-timeline to the larger one.

 Using Maps
Post a topographical map of the eastern U.S. on the bulletin board and encourage the class to turn it into a "war room" map, using colored pushpins to locate the battle sites. Invite students to trace the routes that the armies followed and to identify the geographical obstacles the armies faced.

Revolutionary Women and Children

Women helped write the story of the Revolution. They served on the home front and the battlefront. The experience left many American women thirsting for greater equality.

ASK

1. Some women and children served on the battle lines during the Revolutionary War. What are some of the things they did? *(Women and children cooked for the soldiers and served as spies; some women also fought in battles or served as nurses and did laundry.)*

🌀 **Ponder**
Could the Patriots have succeeded without the help of women and children?

2. How did women who stayed home help out? *(They did work that the men would have done, such as running a business, taking care of a farm.)*

3. What did Mercy Otis Warren and Phyllis Wheatley have in common? *(Help students see that these women used words to try to persuade Loyalists to become Patriots.)*

4. How did some slaves in Massachusetts win their freedom? *(Help students see that the slaves sued in court for their freedom—and won.)*

✔️ **Question Chart**

DISCUSS

1. **Sourcebook:** Read aloud from Source #15 as students follow along. Ask: What is Abigail Adams' point of view regarding the role of women? *(She believes they should have more power.)* Ask: How did women's participation in the war contrast with their rights in colonial America? *(Women fought in the war and did many jobs that men could do, but they had no rights or freedoms—they could not vote, and they were ruled by their fathers and husbands.)*

2. Assign Resource 10 (TG page 84) to help students explore the issue of rights for all Americans.

3. Look at the illustrations of women in this chapter. How would you describe their character or personality, based on the pictures? *(The women seem thoughtful, intelligent, courageous.)*

WRITE

Invite students to write a poem honoring the women and children who helped out in the Revolutionary War. Encourage students to use facts from the chapter as well as their own ideas of how to praise these people.

L I T E R A C Y   L I N K S

Words to Discuss

pension	iniquitous
abomination	blockading
prosperity	

Have students use a dictionary to find the meanings of the two words that describe something undesirable. *(abomination, iniquitous)* Which word means "pay for a retired soldier"? *(pension)* Which word is a synonym for *wealth*? *(prosperity)* If the British were blockading a port, what would they be doing? *(preventing passage in or out)*

Reading Skills
Analyzing Cause and Effect

Draw students' attention to the first sentence of the chapter, "Well, that Declaration did it!" Explain that this short sentence implies a cause-effect relationship—one event caused another event to happen. Ask students the following questions to help them recognize cause-effect relationships implied in this chapter.

• What big thing had the Americans done in 1776? *(signed the Declaration of Independence)*

• What was an important effect of that action? *(The colonies were at war with Great Britain.)*

Explain that causes can have multiple effects—an effect can become a cause of another effect. Ask: What happened when war broke out? *(Colonial men, women, and children began to fight the British.)* ANALYZING

Freedom Fighters

Perhaps nobody understood the limits on equality better than people of African ancestry. Some seized offers of freedom from the British. Others fought to plant the seeds of racial freedom in America.

ASK

1. What job did young James Forten have during the war? *(He was a powder boy, supplying a ship's cannons with gunpowder from below deck.)*
2. What did Forten and other sailors on the *Royal Louis* do that was heroic? *(They captured a British ship.)*
3. As a prisoner, how did Forten show his courage? *(He refused to renounce his country in order to gain his freedom.)*
4. What were Father Escalante and Father Dominguez looking for? *(a great river to the west)*

Ponder
What thoughts might be running through the mind of each person in the picture on page 115?

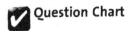 **Question Chart**

DISCUSS

1. How would you feel if you were free and you knew that people just like you were enslaved? How would you feel if you were enslaved and you knew that people just like you were free? *(Help students recognize that the urge for freedom occurred among both free and enslaved African Americans.)*
2. If you had been an African American in Philadelphia in 1776, would you have supported the Patriots or the British? Why? *(Encourage students to consider the viewpoint of both enslaved and free African Americans. Which side promised more—the colonists or the British? Which side was more trustworthy? Which side had ideals that were worth fighting for?)*

WRITE

Ask students to write a two-paragraph biographical sketch of James Forten. Suggest that they use at least one additional resource besides their textbook.

LITERACY LINKS

Words to Discuss

privateer   renounce
powder boy   pueblo

Have students use context to identify the meaning of *powder boy* and *renounce*. Then ask volunteers to look in a dictionary to find the meaning of *privateer* and *pueblo*. Ask other students to use each word in a sentence.

Reading Skills
Recognizing Sequence

Have students read the feature A Failed Journey? on pages 114-115. Point out that the author describes the events in chronological order, using specific dates. Ask students to create a timeline for the events. Then prompt students to create questions based on the timeline, such as, *When did the friars meet the Yutas?* and *About how many months long was their expedition?* Have students exchange and answer questions. QUESTIONING

Skills Connection
Geography

Have students use a map of New Mexico, Colorado, and Utah to identify some of the areas explored by Father Escalante and Father Dominguez.

Soldiers from Everywhere

The cause of liberty drew people from many nations and religions into the conflict. They contributed leadership, money, and, in some cases, their lives.

ASK

1. Why did European soldiers want to join the Patriots? *(There was peace in Europe, and the soldiers didn't know how to do anything but fight. Some believed in liberty and wanted to help.)*

2. What was surprising about the Marquis de Lafayette's request to fight for the Patriots? *(He brought his own ship and soldiers; he asked to fight as a volunteer.)*

3. How did Baron Friedrich von Steuben help the Patriot army? *(He taught the soldiers to be as good as the British troops.)*

4. How did Haym Solomon help America during the Revolution? *(He spied on the British; he gave money to the Continental Congress to help pay for the war.)*

 Ponder
People risked their lives and fortunes to come to America to help fight for independence. Is there somewhere in the world you would be willing to go today to help other people? Where? What would you want to do?

✓ **Question Chart**

DISCUSS

1. What conclusions can you draw about the character traits of the American soldiers? *(Help students recognize that the soldiers were proud, independent-minded, but also fair and respectful once they saw proof of their comrades' ability.)*

2. Compare and contrast the Marquis de Lafayette and Baron von Steuben. *(Lafayette was honest, noble, elegant; von Steuben was boastful, rough, and tough. Both men were intelligent.)*

3. How did many soldiers begin to think of themselves as Americans? *(They or their ancestors had moved about—from Europe to America and within America. They realized that the whole country was under attack, not just part of it.)*

WRITE

Ask students to write a script for a scene between Benjamin Franklin and Baron von Steuben, or between von Steuben and some of the soldiers under his command, or between John Hancock and George Washington (regarding Lafayette's letter of request).

L I T E R A C Y   L I N K S

Words to Discuss

marquis	recruits
drillmaster	dragoon

Ask: In what country would you meet a marquis? *(France)* Have students use context to state the meaning of the word. *(French nobleman)* Have students identify the two words in the compound word *drillmaster*. What meaning does *drill* have here? *(military training)* Have students use a dictionary to find the possible origin of *dragoon (dragon).*

Reading Skills
Analyzing Rhetorical Devices

Refer students to Jefferson's words on page 119. Ask: What words and images does Jefferson use to help the Indians understand the colonists' position and support it? *(little island beyond the great water, Young and weak, say we were their slaves, were determined to be free)* Point out that the Indians were not stupid, but may not have spoken English very well, so Jefferson thought he needed to simplify his presentation. Ask students how they might present the ideas to someone who spoke another language.
ANALYZING

Skills Connection
Geography

Have students use a copy of an outline map of Europe and the colonies to create a visual essay about the contributions of Europeans in the Revolutionary War. Students should identify countries of origin, list names, and briefly describe contributions of Europeans. Display students' work on the bulletin board.

Black Soldiers

Virginians were forced to choose to rebel or to support the king when their royal governor proclaimed "all indentured servants, Negroes, and others . . . free" if they were willing and able to defend the Crown.

ASK

1. What two things did Lord Dunmore proclaim? *(Servants and slaves were free; anyone who didn't support the British was a traitor.)*
2. What happened as a result of Lord Dunmore's proclamation? *(Some blacks joined the British army, some joined the Rebels.)*
3. What happened during the battle at Great Bridge? *(The Rebels beat the Redcoats; black soldiers showed that they could fight as well as anyone.)*
4. What did Thomas Marshall's servant do? *(He tricked the British into thinking the Rebels had only a few hundred soldiers.)*

DISCUSS

1. How did Lord Dunmore's proclamation make life more difficult for both whites and blacks? *(If the whites didn't join the British, they'd be traitors; if the blacks joined, they'd be free, so the proclamation made the conflict between colonial whites and their slaves worse.)* What clue do you have that Lord Dunmore was not sincere in his offer to Virginia's slaves? *(Dunmore did not free his own slaves.)*
2. How can deception be a powerful weapon of war? *(An army needs accurate information about its enemy; if it gets the wrong information, it can make mistakes that lead to its defeat.)*
3. What happened to Norfolk? *(The city was burned.)* How did the burning of Norfolk show that that the war was not just about Americans fighting the British? *(American Patriots fought American Loyalists, and the British fought the Patriots.)*

WRITE

Ask students to write a diary entry that might have been written by a slave, a white indentured servant, a free black person, or a white colonist in response to Lord Dunmore's announcement. Entries should explore the dilemma the person faces.

@ **Ponder**
Why do governments always seem to seize printing presses owned by rebels?

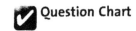 **Question Chart**

L I T E R A C Y   L I N K S

Words to Discuss

imperious   emblazoned
regulars

Challenge students to use Lord Dunmore's speech to determine the meaning of *imperious*. *(haughty, snobbish)* Ask: How would the motto *Liberty to Slaves* have been displayed on the black soldiers' sashes? *(in bold letters)* Have students use a dictionary to determine the meaning of *regulars*.

Reading Skills
Making Inferences

Draw students' attention to the description of Dunmore's departure on page 121. Ask these questions to help students infer why he is leaving Norfolk: What do you know about the war at this point? *(It has begun; rebel forces have won some battles.)* What do you know about Lord Dunmore? *(He's the imperious British governor.)* What can you infer about the number of British troops in Norfolk at this time? *(There are not enough of them for Dunmore to feel secure.)* INFERRING

Skills Connection
Geography

On a map of Africa, have students locate Ethiopia. Explain that while the majority of Africans brought to the United States were from West Africa, at the time *Ethiopia* was a term often used to refer to any black people, a usage that dated back to the days of ancient Greece.

Fighting a War

The opening battles of the war went badly for Washington. His strategy rested less on pursuing victory than on avoiding capture.

ASK

1. What was the condition of Washington's army? *(His soldiers were poorly clothed, poorly paid, and poorly armed; some froze to death during the winter, and some deserted the army.)*

2. What happened between Washington's army and the British in New York? *(The British sent troops by ship; the Rebel army retreated because they did not have much experience.)*

3. What good luck did Washington have? *(A thick fog and some sharp-eyed fishermen helped him escape from the British.)*

4. Who were the Hessians? *(German soldiers hired by the British to fight against the Rebels)*

Ponder
Would hiring mercenaries be a good idea for countries at war today? Why or why not?

Question Chart

DISCUSS

1. At this point in the war, what conclusions can you draw about the kind of military leader General Washington was? *(He was calm and commanded respect, but he does not seem to have trained his soldiers very well or done much to get them the food, clothing, and pay that they needed.)*

2. What caused some Americans who were unsure which side to be on to become Patriots? *(They were furious when they saw that the British forces included soldiers from Germany who were paid to fight for the British.)*

WRITE

Have student pairs role-play being a newspaper reporter and General Washington. The reporter should prepare a set of questions about the soldiers and the war; the "General" should be prepared to describe the situation he and his soldiers face. Invite students to present their interview in written or oral form.

L I T E R A C Y L I N K S

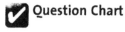

Words to Discuss

retreat   Hessians
mercenaries

Direct students to use context to state the meaning of these words. *(retreat—withdraw; Hessians— soldiers from Hesse, in Germany; mercenaries—hired soldiers)*

Reading Skills
Predicting

Before reading the chapter, invite students to scan the main title, feature titles, illustrations, and captions. Encourage students to use what they have learned about the war so far and what they see in Chapter 27 to make predictions about how the American army will do in its next encounters with the British. Ask students to identify specific clues that helped them make their predictions. *(Possible responses: The Americans will lose because they are outnumbered; the Americans will win because they are tough, determined, and will be joined by the French.)* PREDICTING

Meeting Individual Needs
Enrichment

Challenge students to paraphrase General Howe's assessment of the American forces on page 124 and to contrast the Americans' situation on Long Island with their situation on Sullivan's Island.

Howe Billy Wished France Wouldn't Join In

The American victory at Saratoga changed the war. Sensing that the Americans could win, the French jumped in on their side.

ASK

1. What luck did Washington have in the winter of 1776? *(General Howe stopped fighting and settled in New York City.)*
2. How did Washington fool the British at Princeton? *(He left a few troops at Trenton, marched his men to Princeton, and defeated the British force there.)*
3. What was the effect of Washington's small victories? *(They raised the Patriots' morale.)*
4. How did the Patriots beat the British at Fort Edward? *(They used guerrilla tactics.)*
5. What happened at Saratoga? *(The Americans, led by General Gates, defeated the British.)*

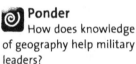
Ponder
How does knowledge of geography help military leaders?

Question Chart

DISCUSS

1. The British have surrendered at Saratoga. What do you predict will happen next? *(Possible responses: The war will continue; Britain will send more soldiers; the Americans will become more confident and will win.)* What facts or clues help you make your predictions? *(Possible responses: The author says the war wasn't over; the French have joined the Americans; Americans use guerrilla tactics; Americans outnumber the British.)*
2. Assign Resource 11 (TG page 85) to help students assess the costs of the war.
3. Have students read General Burgoyne's words on page 129; then have them read the author's summary. Explain that a summary includes the key ideas but is shorter than the original text. Ask students to summarize the paragraph beginning *Saratoga edges . . .* at the bottom of page 128. *(Gates and Kosciuszko created a trap for Burgoyne.)*

WRITE

Have students imagine they are either General Gates or General Burgoyne after the battle of Saratoga. Ask students to write a letter that the general would write to his friends and family about the battle.

L I T E R A C Y   L I N K S

Words to Discuss

oath of allegiance   guerrilla
sniped

Discuss with students what they do when they say the Pledge of Allegiance. Ask students to draw conclusions about what the 3,000 Americans in New Jersey did when they swore an oath of allegiance to the king. *(swore loyalty)* Have students use context to get the meaning of *sniped* and *guerrilla*. *(shot from behind trees; attacked in a random way)* Ask: In what earlier war did these tactics play a role?

Reading Skills
Identifying Main Idea and Details

Draw students' attention to the first paragraph on page 127, beginning *But George. . . .* Have students read the paragraph and identify the main idea. *(But George Washington was no quitter.)* Ask: Where does the main idea appear? *(at the beginning of the paragraph)* Help students recognize that the remaining sentences are details that support the main idea. Point out that the main idea does not always appear at the beginning of a paragraph. Have

students read the last paragraph on page 127 and identify the main idea and its location. *(And American morale needed help; second sentence)* INFERRING

Valley Forge to Vincennes

The hardships of war gave Washington a battle-tested army. After Valley Forge, these troops began a campaign to sweep the British and their mercenaries from their land.

ASK

1. How did Washington's army change after it spent the winter at Valley Forge? *(It had new strength, pride, and self-confidence.)*

2. What are three things that helped the soldiers survive the winter at Valley Forge? *(Washington's calmness and dignity, his wife's good will, and Von Steuben's hard work and good humor)*

3. Why were the Indians angry? *(Their lands were being taken from them and their way of life threatened.)*

4. What was the aim of the Indian fighters? *(to drive the Indians west so that settlers could take their land)*

◎ **Ponder**
How can going through a bad period help a person or group of people become stronger? Think about examples from literature, movies, and television, or from your own life.

☑ **Question Chart**

DISCUSS

1. No battles were fought at Valley Forge, so why is it important in the Revolutionary War? *(The soldiers were drilled and trained. They survived very harsh conditions and developed pride, self-confidence, and military skill.)*

2. Why did fighting take place west of the Appalachians? *(The British paid Native Americans to attack American settlers. The Americans wanted to protect themselves and throw the British out of this rich region.)*

3. Assign Resource 12 (TG page 86) to help students identify important points in the war so far.

WRITE

Suggest that students develop ideas for a TV episode about the chapter events. One group might develop ideas for the Valley Forge episode, another group might develop ideas for the Vincennes episode. Students should identify and describe characters, dialogue, narration, settings, and events to be presented in a half-hour segment.

LITERACY LINKS

Words to Discuss

> mutiny   quartermaster
> serfs

Have students use a dictionary to find the word derived from the Latin for *move. (mutiny)* Explain how a *mutiny* is a forceful move against military authority. Draw students' attention to the compound word *quartermaster*, and to the multiple meanings of *quarter*. Students should use context to determine the meaning of *quartermaster* and *serfs*. *(person in charge of supplies; people who are like slaves)*

Meeting Individual Needs
Enrichment

The beginning of this chapter refers to Washington's defeats at the battles of Brandywine and Germantown. Students with an interest in military history might research these battles and present their findings to the class.

Skills Connection
History/Science

Invite students to research information on Bushnell's Turtle submarine. Students should describe its features and the scientific principles that enabled it to remain submerged.

THINKING ABOUT THE THEMES

The following questions will help students relate the book's themes to the content of Part 5. You may wish to use the questions for classroom discussion or have students answer them in written form.

1. Describe the effects that the Declaration of Independence had on the conflict between the American colonies and Great Britain. *(The conflict became a war to found a nation; it became a war to prove that people could rule themselves; it became a people's war.)*

2. In what ways was the Revolutionary War a people's war? *(The war's leaders, such as George Washington, were popular figures; ordinary people—white and black, men, women, and children—participated in the war.)*

3. During the war, what were some of the changes occurring among people in the colonies? *(Some of the women and African Americans were asking for the same rights that white men had; some colonists were moving westward; immigrant Americans were learning to get along with each other; African American soldiers were showing they could fight as well as anyone; the colonial army became stronger.)*

4. Draw students' attention to the themes that have been posted around the room. Give them the opportunity to explore the relevance of these themes to Part 5. Accept choices that are supported by sound reasoning.

ASSESSING PART 5

Use Check-Up 5 (TG page 72) to assess student learning.

NOTE FROM JOY HAKIM

Historian/educator Paul Cagnon says a proper history text should provide "lively chronological narrative and regular pauses in that narrative, to look in depth at particular people, events, ideas, and turning points. Neither alone is enough. Students need the large story over time to see the place and significance of topics selected for study in depth." I agree.

PROJECTS AND ACTIVITIES

▶ Battle Lines

Have volunteers continue work on the war-room map begun in Introducing Part 5. Other students can create text to accompany the map by answering these questions: Where did most of the major battles occur in 1775? *(New England states)* 1776-1777? *(Middle states)* Have students write reasons why the fighting shifted regions.

▶ Revolutionary Posters

Have small groups of students design posters celebrating the contributions of women, children, and African Americans in the American Revolution. Some posters could focus on participation in battles; others could focus on tasks away from the battlefield, such as running family farms or businesses, making bullets, or sewing shirts for troops.

▶ Spain Helps Clark

Ask students to research Bernardo de Galvez, a Spanish official in New Orleans who supplied some of the gunpowder that helped George Rogers Clark take Vincennes. He also sent herds of longhorns to feed Washington's hungry troops. Have students present their findings in an oral report called *Spanish Hero of the Revolution*. Students who speak Spanish could write a tribute to Galvez in Spanish.

★★ FACTS TO SHARE ★★

Another woman who distinguished herself in the Revolution was 16-year-old Sybil Luddington. On the night of April 26, 1777, a messenger rode up to tell her father, a colonel of the local militia, that an attack was about to take place on Patriot munitions stored at Danbury, Connecticut. The messenger and his horse were too exhausted to carry the alarm further, so Sybil volunteered. She rode 40 miles that night, spreading the alarm to the surrounding militia.

6

Experiments with Independence

In 1774, a 19-year-old New Yorker named Alexander Hamilton wrote: "The only distinction between freedom and slavery consists in this: In the former state, a man is governed by laws to which he has given his consent, either in person or by his representative: In the latter, he is governed by the will of another." A popular slogan in the 1770s put the matter more simply: "Where annual elections end, slavery begins." Even as bullets flew, Americans put their political beliefs into practice. Part 6 tells these first tentative steps in the creation of the world's first federal republic.

SETTING GOALS

The goals for students in Part 6 are to:
- explain problems in designing a government for the country.
- understand how Americans tried to safeguard their rights.
- identify the weaknesses of the Articles of Confederation.
- describe how lands west of the Appalachians became part of the new nation.

GETTING INTERESTED

1. Ask students to brainstorm ideas about the word *constitution*. You might write their ideas on the board in a word web. Guide students in concluding that a constitution is a set of laws that shapes the way a government operates. It does so by stating which powers the government has over the people and which it does not. Explain that the states were creating written constitutions, which had never been done before. Ask: What do you think the colonists wanted their constitution to say?

2. Elicit from students that, because of its colonial background, each American state was like a miniature country: each had its own money, army, form of government, and so on. Have students make predictions about how effective the Continental Congress would be in governing the new "nation."

Working with Timelines
On the class timeline, have students enter 1781, 1783, and 1784. Tell students that each date might be considered the end of the Revolutionary War. Ask them to look for details supporting each date as they read this part. *(The dates are for the Battle of Yorktown, the signing of the Treaty of Paris, and the ratification of the Treaty of Paris by Congress, respectively.)*

Using Maps
Refer students to the map on page 148 and have them identify the two major areas about which the Continental Congress had to make decisions. Guide students in recognizing the location of British and Spanish territory. Ask: What problems do you think the Congress will face as it decides how to govern the new nation? *(Arguments about boundaries, numbers of people to be represented, slavery, Indians)*

The States Write Constitutions

The ideas that shaped the Constitution of the United States were first expressed in written form in documents produced at the state level. Two broad concerns guided the authors' pens: protection from abuses of power and guarantees of liberty.

ASK

1. What idea was everyone talking about after the war? *(liberty)*
2. What did the state leaders worry about? *(power)*
3. What are the three main branches of government? *(legislative, executive, judicial)*
4. What did the writers of state constitutions try to do about the main branches of government? *(separate them; balance them)*
5. What happened when the Massachusetts constitution stated that "All men are born free and equal"? *(Slaves asked the courts for their freedom and got it.)*
6. What was new in the Virginia Bill of Rights? *(freedom of religion)*

⊙ Ponder
John Dickinson's copy of the Pennsylvania constitution on page 137 is covered with changes. Why was rewriting like this so important to the final constitutions?

✔ Question Chart

DISCUSS

1. What does *separation of powers* mean? *(It means that the government's power is divided among different branches.)* Why did it become part of the state constitutions? *(The people who wrote the constitutions hoped this would keep one group from gaining too much power.)*
2. Summarize the author's thoughts on why the information about state constitutional conventions is not boring. *(She thinks they were an exciting experiment because no country had ever created constitutions like these.)*

WRITE

Have students in groups of four or five imagine themselves as writers of a state constitution. Have them discuss at least four of the items listed on page 136 and create a draft constitution that explains how these issues would be resolved for their state. Encourage students to keep in mind the social and political attitudes of the time.

LITERACY LINKS

Words to Discuss

separation of powers
legislative branch
executive branch
judicial branch

Have students use context to define each phrase. The text uses the analogy of a tree to describe the governments; challenge students to come up with their own analogy, such as forks of a river, legs of a stool, and so on.

Reading Skills
Analyzing Text Features

Call students' attention to the list of argued points for the state constitutions on page 136. Discuss: How is the type different, and what does that tell you? *(The type is italic, which means the information is important.)* How does the list help you? *(It presents the points in an easy-to-read way.)* ANALYZING

Meeting Individual Needs
English Language Learners

To help students understand the meanings of *executive branch*, *legislative branch*, and *judicial branch*, have them draw the tree described on page 135 and label its branches with the appropriate names. Then describe what each branch does in the government. Ask students to repeat or paraphrase your descriptions below each branch on the diagram.

More About Choices

In the Far West, Spanish settlers were leaving their mark on lands destined to become part of the United States. In the East, individuals such as Mary Katherine Goddard set precedents that would one day be shared by all people who called themselves American.

ASK

1. Why did Spain send people to take over land that belonged to the Indians? *(to keep the Russians from colonizing California)* What was the result? *(The Indians' way of life was destroyed.)*

2. How did Henry Knox help the Revolutionary Army? *(He figured out how to move cannons from Fort Ticonderoga to Boston.)*

3. Who published the first copies of the Declaration of Independence? *(Mary Katherine Goddard)*

4. How did it become established that journalists could keep their sources secret? *(The governor of Maryland protected Mary Katherine Goddard when she refused to tell the name of the author of an article she published.)*

⊚ Ponder
Should journalists be permitted to keep their sources secret? Why or why not?

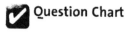 **Question Chart**

DISCUSS

1. Some historians say that the Revolution was also a civil war—a war between citizens of the same country. How does the story of Lucy Knox support this idea? *(The Revolution tore her family apart, dividing Patriots and Loyalists.)*

2. Discuss: How does the story of Mary Katherine Goddard show that Americans still had a long way to go to fulfill their ideals? *(Elicit from students the inequities reflected in her story.)*

WRITE

Invite student pairs to imagine that one of them lives in the eastern American colonies and the other lives in one of the Spanish settlements of the West. Have students compose letters to each other describing the events that are taking place.

LITERACY LINKS

Words to Discuss

contagious   satire
artillery

Discuss the meaning of *contagious*. Ask: You know how a disease can be contagious; how can an *idea* be contagious? *(It catches on in people's minds.)* Have students use context to identify the meaning of *artillery* and *satire. (cannons, big guns; a form of humor)*

Reading Skills
Analyzing Graphic Aids

Using the map on page 139, have students identify the meaning of the symbol for a Spanish mission. *(The cross represents the Roman Catholic Church.)* Then have them analyze the locations of the missions. Ask: Near what kinds of landforms were the missions built? *(In California and New Mexico, they were built along coastal areas and in mountainous areas; some*

were built in flatlands in New Mexico and Texas.) Was the Spanish population of the West greater or less than that of the English colonies in the East? Why? *(Less, because the missions were small and spread out, and the Spaniards did not have large numbers of slaves.)*
ANALYZING/INFERRING

When It's Over, Shout Hooray

With the help of France, the Americans finally backed the British into a corner at Yorktown. The fife and drum played a tune that summed up the American victory: "The World Turned Upside Down."

ASK

1. How did the colonists match the British army's might? *(They had a strong belief in their cause.)*
2. Why did the British shift the war to the south? *(to try to break a stalemate or stand-off)*
3. What happened in the battle at Yorktown? *(Help students recognize that with the help of the French—both on land and at sea—the colonists surrounded and defeated the British.)*
4. What happened as a result of the colonial victory at Yorktown? *(A new nation started to form, based on freedom and equality.)*

Ponder
Weather conditions play an important role in any war. How might the weather have brought about a different result at Yorktown?

DISCUSS

1. Why was the stalemate following Saratoga good for the Americans? *(It showed that the Americans had not given up and were not defeated; it gave them time to plan and strengthen themselves.)*
2. Why do you think "The World Turned Upside Down" was a good song for the British surrender? *(The strongest power in the world had been defeated by one of the weakest.)*
3. Summarize the war after Saratoga. *(The British shifted to the south and won several battles, but the Americans' spirit was strong. The Americans were joined by the French and marched to Yorktown. At Yorktown they learned that the French navy had turned back the English supply ships. French and American armies defeated the British.)*

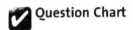 **Question Chart**

WRITE

Ask students to write a newspaper account of the Battle of Yorktown. Articles should include descriptions of key events and people.

L I T E R A C Y   L I N K S

Words to Discuss

stalemate   bay
dashing

Direct students to use context to define *stalemate*. *(a draw; even)* Ask: Who are some dashing figures in today's world? *(Responses will vary.)* What are some of the meanings of *bay*? *(waterway, area for a car, kind of horse, kind of tree or shrub)*

Reading Strategies
Analyzing Political Cartoons

Ask students to use a magnifying glass to examine the cartoon on page 142. Ask the following questions: What two things does the female on the right represent? *(Great Britain; mother of the colonies)* Who does Washington represent? *(the colonies, Britain's children)* What words in the balloons are clues to the meaning? *(children, parents)* Guide students in recognizing how the drawings and words of the other characters represent, from left to right, Germany, France, and Holland. ANALYZING

Skills Connection
Geography

Using Resource 13 (TG page 87), have students trace the course of events leading to the British surrender at Yorktown and discuss how geography played a role in the American victory.

Experimenting with a Nation

When the Revolution ended, few Americans talked of the United States. Unity took the form of the loose association of states created by the Articles of Confederation. Its weaknesses paved the way for a new government—a federal republic.

ASK

1. What task did the Americans face after the war? *(building a nation)*
2. What issues did the states argue about? *(taxes and boundaries)*
3. What was the first constitution called? *(Articles of Confederation)*
4. What did the states fear? *(giving too much power to Congress and to the President of the Congress)*

 Ponder
What might have happened if the states had not tried to form a national government in 1781?

 **Question Chart**

DISCUSS

1. What was the Articles of Confederation and why did it fail? *(It was the first constitution of the United States. American citizens were afraid of a strong government, so the Articles gave the national government almost no power. The national government could not collect taxes to pay its bills; it was not supported by the states; it gave each state only one vote, regardless of the state's population.)*

2. **Sourcebook:** Read aloud from Source #16 (for example, from Articles II, V, and IX) as students follow along. Have students identify how the Articles limited the central government's powers. Ask: Why might the country have been called the "Disunited States" in 1781? *(Each state had its own money, ways of taxing, boundary squabbles, and rebellious citizens. The states were independent rather than unified.)*

WRITE

Ask students to imagine that George Washington had proclaimed himself king. Have them write a paragraph telling how the United States might be different today as a result.

LITERACY LINKS

Words to Discuss

**supply and demand
inflation
Articles of Confederation**

Have students use context to define *supply and demand* and *inflation*. Ask for other examples of items that are costly because they are rare, cheap because they are plentiful, or that have inflated prices. Have student find the appropriate meanings of *article* and *confederation* in a dictionary.

Reading Skills
Analyzing Visual Aids

Have students identify the images in the cartoon on page 150. Ask: What seems to be the cartoonist's point of view about how the American states will behave toward Great Britain? *(The cartoonist seems to think the states will make peace with Britain, as shown by the olive branch.)* ANALYZING

Skills Connection
Geography

Direct students to the map on page 148 and have them identify which states claimed western lands beyond the borders of the original 13 colonies. Have students draw conclusions about how the states were getting along in view of these claims, and how the United States might be different if the states had actually got the land they claimed.

Looking Northwest

The one triumph of the national government under the Articles of Confederation was the passage of the Northwest Ordinance. This law helped ensure the orderly expansion of the United States by allowing territories to become new states on an equal footing with the original states.

ASK

1. What was the Northwest Ordinance? *(a law that allowed territories to become states)*

2. Before a territory could become a state, what had to happen? *(The territory had to be divided into townships; then groups of towns became states.)*

3. Why were Native Americans being pushed from their lands? *(The British could no longer protect them from the settlers who were moving westward.)*

4. What did the Northwest Ordinance allow in the new territories? *(basic freedoms, such as freedom of religion; education)* What did it not allow? *(slavery, involuntary servitude)*

5. What did the Northwest Ordinance have that the state constitutions also had? *(a bill of rights)*

◎ Ponder
Are citizens today as educated as they should be? What changes, if any, would you make to improve schools?

DISCUSS

1. Refer students to the list of issues that Americans argued about when they created state constitutions (page 138). Ask: How well do you think the Northwest Ordinance dealt with these issues? *(Encourage students to find in Chapter 33 specific references to each issue. Help students recognize that the Ordinance dealt directly with several of them.)*

2. **Sourcebook:** Read aloud from Source #21 as students follow along. Have students identify freedoms and prohibitions stated in the Northwest Ordinance.

3. Why is it important for citizens to be educated if they want to govern themselves? *(Students should recognize that education gives citizens information and the ability to think for themselves, which gives them power to make decisions.)*

✔ Question Chart

WRITE

Have students write a two-paragraph essay titled *What Was Right About the Northwest Ordinance*. Encourage students to describe the purpose, features, and effects of the Ordinance.

LITERACY LINKS

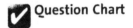

Words to Discuss

ordinance   township
Conestoga
involuntary servitude

Explain that *Conestoga* is an eponym—the name of a real place or person that becomes the name of something associated with that place or person. Conestoga wagons were made in the Conestoga Valley, Pennsylvania. Have students use context and a dictionary to determine the other words' meanings.

Reading Skills
Making Inferences

Ask students to compare the statements by Jefferson and Berkeley (margin note) on page 153. Ask: How are these points of view different? *(Jefferson believed citizens had to be educated in order to be free; Berkeley believed education was dangerous for citizens.)* What can you infer about Berkeley's nationality? *(He was probably a British royal governor.)* What can you infer about the kind of society each person might view as ideal? *(Jefferson would like a democratic society; Berkeley would like a monarchy or aristocracy.)* INFERRING

A Man with Ideas

Thomas Jefferson was, among other things, an inventor, architect, author, and visionary political leader. The idea of separation of church and state owes its origins to Thomas Jefferson and his friend James Madison.

ASK

1. In what two documents that you've studied so far do you find many of Thomas Jefferson's ideas? *(the Declaration of Independence and the Northwest Ordinance)*
2. What was odd about Jefferson and the issue of slavery? *(He was opposed to slavery, yet refused to free his own slaves.)*
3. What unique idea did Jefferson have about religion and government? *(Religion and government should be separate; citizens should have religious freedom.)*
4. What school did Jefferson create? *(University of Virginia)*

 Ponder
Why didn't Jefferson free his slaves?

✔ **Question Chart**

DISCUSS

1. What role did education play in Thomas Jefferson's early life? *(His parents sought out good teachers; his parents and teachers encouraged him; he met educated people who became his friends.)* Do you think he would have become a great man without the early experiences he had? *(Help students infer that his education was very important to his development.*
2. Assign Resource 14 (TG page 88) to help students organize ideas and information about Jefferson.
3. **Sourcebook:** Read aloud from Source #19 ("Be it enacted . . .") and Source 21 (Article 1) and have students compare the ideas stated in Jefferson's *Virginia Statute* and in the Northwest Ordinance.

WRITE

Have pairs of students collaborate on writing a dialogue between Thomas Jefferson and Mary Katherine Goddard. Topics for discussion should be the Declaration of Independence, women's role in colonial society, and slavery.

L I T E R A C Y   L I N K S

Words to Discuss

intellectual   decimal system
piedmont
separation of church and state

Have students use context to define these terms. *(intellectual*—idea-centered person; *decimal system*—number system based on tens; *piedmont*—foothills; *separation of church and state*—government cannot tell citizens how to worship)

Meeting Individual Needs
English Language Learners
Students will benefit from studying the key words with more-fluent classmates. Student pairs should focus on pronunciation of the words as well as on understanding the meanings.

Skills Connection
History/Science

Direct students to the Cow Cure feature on page 156, and suggest that they research the development of the smallpox vaccine after Jenner's discovery. Students should try to find out what happened to the number of incidents of smallpox between 1741 and 1979, and why smallpox came back into the news early in the 21st century. Encourage students to report their findings to the class or to create a bulletin board display.

SUMMARIZING PART 6

THINKING ABOUT THE THEMES

The following questions will help students relate the book's themes to the content of Part 6. You may wish to use the questions for classroom discussion or have students answer them in written form.

1. Describe some of the steps the states took toward nation-building. What were some of the stumbling blocks along the way? *(Each state wrote a constitution, but the states argued amongst themselves over boundaries and taxes; the states approved the Articles of Confederation, but they did not give Congress the power it needed to do a good job; Congress passed the Northwest Ordinance which helped territories become states, but the ordinance did not protect the Indians from settlers.)*

2. What were some of the conflicts involving the role of women and African Americans in the new nation? Give examples. *(Women still had no rights. Mary Katherine Goddard lost her job as postmistress to a man, even though she was supported by 200 businessmen; slavery was not allowed in the Northwest Territories, but remained in some states. Jefferson spoke out against slavery, but did not free his own slaves.)*

3. Compare and contrast the government of the Americans before and after the Revolution. *(Before the Revolution, the American colonies were ruled by the powerful British government. Although they all had representative colonial assemblies, they also had royal governors backed by British soldiers, and were subject to laws enacted by the British government without their consent. After the Revolution, the states' governments were run by the citizens. The central government was much weaker than the state governments.)*

4. Draw students' attention to the themes that have been posted around the room. Give them the opportunity to explore the relevance of these themes to Part 6. Accept choices that are supported by sound reasoning.

ASSESSING PART 6

Use Check-Up 6 (TG page 73) to assess student learning.

PROJECTS AND ACTIVITIES

▶ Connecting with State Constitutions

Assign small groups of students to locate a copy of your state constitution. Ask students to find and summarize the parts of the constitution that describe the legislative, judicial, and executive branches. Ask students to summarize at least one article in the state bill of rights. Have students share their information.

▶ Visualizing Life in a Spanish Colony

Direct students to the picture and map on pages 138 and 139. Suggest that students use these visuals to brainstorm a description of daily life in a Spanish colony. Students should consider categories such as religion, housing, travel, obtaining food, and relations with Native Americans. Ask students to present their ideas as a "reality" television show.

▶ Fans of Jefferson

Invite students to write a script for a three-minute docudrama on the life of Thomas Jefferson. Encourage students to use information from previous Parts as well.

▶ Other Voices

Suggest that students produce a panel discussion among Lucy Flucker Knox, Mary Katherine Goddard, Mohawk Joseph Brant, a slave from Massachusetts, and Thomas Jefferson about the state of the new nation. Students should role play the individuals and record their comments. One student should act as moderator.

★ ★ FACTS TO SHARE ★ ★

Jefferson is also thought to have introduced to America the knowledge from France of how to make ice cream. He was certainly one of the first to serve it at a state dinner. He served it in the middle of a crisp hot pastry, which was perhaps the nation's first ice cream sandwich. Today, Americans consume 20 pounds of ice cream per capita each year.

Creating a New Nation

In 1787, delegates to the Constitutional Convention rolled up their sleeves and created the Constitution of the United States. The document was shaped by conflicts and by the compromises that resolved them. It included imperfections born of the times. But the Constitution also gave Americans the tools for change. Part 7 tells how the Framers drafted a blueprint for republican government.

SETTING GOALS

The goals for students in Part 7 are to:
- identify the major step the nation took to revamp its government.
- describe the roles of the major figures who created the Constitution.
- explain the major points of debate and the compromises that went into creating and adopting the Constitution.

GETTING INTERESTED

1. Introduce Part 7 by writing *Where We Stand So Far* on the chalkboard. Invite students to create a picture of the situation in the United States in the mid-1780s, by answering questions like these: What have we achieved so far? What problems do we still have to face? Guide students in recognizing that despite defeating the British, creating state constitutions, and creating the Articles of Confederation, there is only a weak national government and troubles among the states.

2. Tell students that the Constitution of the United States has been called a "bundle of compromises." Discuss the word *compromise* and ask students why there is likely to be a lot of it as the delegates try to create a constitution. You might suggest that students create a list of key compromises as they read the Part.

 Working with Timelines
Point out to the class that they are about to study the last Part of Book Three, and ask them to use the class and individual timelines to review the journey they have made as time travelers, beginning with the trial of Peter Zenger in 1735. Ask them to make predictions about the outcome of the journey in 1791. What changes will take place? What conflicts will be resolved? What conflicts will remain?

 Using Maps
Have students study a historical map of Philadelphia and locate the streets and landmark buildings mentioned in the text of Chapters 35 and 36. (See the map reproduced on page 166.) Ask what geographical features of Philadelphia might have contributed to its becoming an important and popular city? *(location between two rivers, protected inland location yet with access to the sea)*

A Philadelphia Welcome

Led by James Madison, the Virginians traveled to the Constitutional Convention armed with ideas for change. Instead of revising the Articles of Confederation, delegates found themselves debating a new proposal, the so-called Virginia Plan.

ASK

1. Why do you think the delegates chose to meet in Philadelphia? *(It was an exciting, modern city—the largest in North America.)*
2. What qualities did Madison have that made him a good delegate? *(He was intelligent, hard working, scholarly, and sensible.)*
3. What did Madison think the convention should do about the Articles of Confederation? *(throw them out and write a new constitution)*
4. Whose help did Madison ask for in planning the convention? *(Thomas Jefferson's)*
5. How did the Virginia Plan help the delegates? *(The plan made it easy for them to begin their discussions because they had something to talk about.)*

DISCUSS

1. What was the "American crisis" that Edmund Randolph referred to? *(Possible responses: The Articles of Confederation did not work as a plan to unify the states; there was still no central government; there was no national leader.)*
2. Remind students that they learned a great deal about Thomas Jefferson in the previous chapter. Ask: What similarities and differences do you see between James Madison and Thomas Jefferson? *(Possible responses: Both were from Virginia Piedmont region, both received a good education; both were idea-centered people, or intellectuals; both were scholarly; both disliked slavery but benefited from the labor of slaves; both were popular. Madison was short, Jefferson was tall; Jefferson had a wider range of interests and achievements.)*

Ponder
Imagine a conversation between John Bartram and Benjamin Franklin about the need for a scientific expedition. What would the goals be? Why would it be important?

✔ Question Chart

WRITE

Have students imagine they are James Madison as he writes to Thomas Jefferson in Paris. Suggest students write a letter explaining what Madison has on his mind (for example, getting rid of the Articles of Confederation, coming up with a new plan of government) and asking Jefferson for help.

LITERACY LINKS

Words to Discuss

constitutional convention
imposing
Virginia Plan

Have students create a word web with *constitutional convention* at the center. Invite them to add details they've learned about the convention. Have them use a dictionary to look up the meaning of *imposing* and to identify a synonym. Have students use context to describe the Virginia Plan.

Reading Skills
Identifying Sensory Details

Ask students to reread the first four paragraphs of the chapter and identify examples of description that appeal to the different senses. *(sight—straight, broad avenues, evenly spaced water pumps; sound—clattering horses' hoofs, language from the jail, cheering crowds; touch/sight—dusty, muddy roads)* VISUALIZING

Skills Connection
History/Science

The Royal Society is the oldest and foremost scientific organization in the world. It was founded in 1660 as the Royal Society of London for Improving Natural Knowledge. Ask students to research information about the society, including its aims, membership, and some of its accomplishments. Students may wish to go the society's Website at *http://www.royalsoc.ac.uk*. Have researchers present their findings to the class.

Summer in Philly

In public, delegates eagerly enjoyed the charms of Philadelphia. Meanwhile, ordinary Philadelphians knew nothing of the bitter conflicts taking place each day behind the locked doors of the Pennsylvania State House.

ASK

1. How would you summarize the author's description of Philadelphia in the summer of 1787? *(hot, smelly, unsanitary)*
2. Why did the Congress meet in secret? *(Help students recognize that the delegates wanted to be able to change their minds, if necessary, before the document was finalized, and they didn't want outsiders to criticize or pick apart the document before it was finished.)*
3. How do we know what happened during the Convention? *(James Madison took notes.)*
4. What did Sir Isaac Newton, Benjamin Franklin, Thomas Jefferson, James Madison, Benjamin Rush, and David Rittenhouse have in common? *(They were all scientists or interested in science.)*

 Ponder
While Congress was meeting in secret, what were ordinary people wondering about what was going on?

 **Question Chart**

DISCUSS

1. Draw students' attention to the Behind Closed Doors feature and to the author's questions in the last paragraph. Have students discuss these questions: Were the delegates' reasons for secrecy good enough? *(Responses will vary.)* What are the advantages of private discussions? *(Possible response: people can argue and change their minds; they can talk about technical matters.)* What are the dangers of closed lawmaking? *(Possible response: lawmakers may become too powerful.)*
2. Do you think the delegates' interest in science had any affect on their ideas at the Convention? Why or why not? *(Possible response: Yes. The delegates were guided by ideas of order, logic, and balance, which are also ideas in science.)*

WRITE

Write a journal or diary entry that one of the delegates might have written about a day in Philadelphia in the summer of 1787. In your entry, use descriptions that appeal to the senses.

LITERACY LINKS

Words to Discuss

median   friction
Framers

Ask students to use context in the features on pages 162, 163, and 165 to define the words. Then ask students to use each word in an original sentence.

Reading Skills
Recognizing Contrasts

Ask students to identify places in the text where the author contrasts conditions or events of the past with conditions and events today. You may wish to have students create a two-column chart titled *Then and Now* to record these contrasts. Ask students to draw conclusions about why the author included these contrasts.
CONNECTING

Meeting Individual Needs
Enrichment

Students may wish to discover why none of the firebrands of the Revolution—Samuel Adams, Patrick Henry, or Thomas Paine—were delegates to the Constitutional Convention. Ask researchers to find out what happened to each of them and why they were no longer closely involved with setting up a national government. Encourage students to share their findings with the class.

A Slap on the Back

The issue of power again divided the delegates. Some wanted strong state governments; others wanted a strong national government. Out of the debate came a compromise: a federal system with shared power.

ASK

1. How did John Rutledge's ideas about property and rights differ from James Wilson's ideas? *(Rutledge believed that property was the most important thing; Wilson believed that individual rights were more important than property.)*

2. Why did some people not believe in democracy in 1787? *(They thought only the wealthy and educated should vote; they were afraid of mobs.)*

3. How did Gouverneur Morris contribute to the Constitution? *(He polished the language when the Constitution was almost finished.)*

4. What kind of government did Alexander Hamilton want? *(He wanted a government like England's, with a king-like president and a strong central government.)*

5. How is a confederation different from a federation? *(In a confederation, partners hold all the power and the central government is weak; in a federation, power is balanced between a central government and state governments.)*

 **Ponder**
What might happen if one or both of the Mollys (Chapter 22) showed up for dinner at the home of Eliza Powel?

☑ **Question Chart**

DISCUSS

1. Have students compare and contrast the delegates described in this chapter. You may want to have students construct in their notebooks or on the chalkboard a *Who's Who* cast of characters for the Constitutional Convention. Students should briefly describe each delegate's personality, physical appearance, and political ideas. Invite students to continue the list as they work through the remaining chapters.

2. In what ways was the government created by the delegates a compromise? *(Possible response: The central government was not as strong as some delegates wanted, and the states' powers were not as great as other delegates wanted. Neither side got everything it wanted.)*

WRITE

Invite students to write a parody of a social evening at the home of one of the rich Philadelphians, using the author's descriptions as a reference.

L I T E R A C Y   L I N K S

Words to Discuss

confederation	federation
federal	federalism

Guide students in making a graphic organizer to show how these words and their definitions are related. The organizer might be a Venn diagram of three overlapping circles with the word *federal* (and its definition) in common. Each circle should include the definition of the appropriate term. Then ask students to discuss the similarities and differences among the meanings.

Reading Skills
Analyzing Point of View

Refer the class to the Sense Being Preferable to Sound feature (page 171). Ask: What did the town do and what did it want from Franklin? *(It named itself after Franklin and it wanted him to pay for a bell for a steeple for its meeting house.)* What was Franklin's view of what should be done? *(He thought the town should start a library to educate its citizens rather than build a steeple.)* ANALYZING

Creating Questions

Ask students to infer what groups of people among Philadelphia's population are not described in this chapter. Then ask students to write questions that the author might have answered concerning these groups. QUESTIONING

Roger to the Rescue

Another conflict over power erupted when big and little states battled over representation. Roger Sherman settled the matter with a compromise that created a bicameral legislature.

ASK

1. What did the Virginia Plan say about the number of congressmen from each state? *(that the number should be decided by the population of each state)*
2. Why did some delegates not like the Virginia Plan? *(The larger states got the most representatives in Congress.)*
3. What did the New Jersey Plan say about the number of congressmen from each state? *(All states should have the same number, regardless of population.)*
4. What was Roger Sherman's compromise? *(The Congress should have two houses. Representation in the House of Representatives should be based on the population of each state; representation in the Senate should be equal for each state.)*

 Ponder
If the delegates really believed in democracy, why did some of them seem to object to rule by the majority?

 **Question Chart**

DISCUSS

1. Why didn't the little states want the big states to have most of the representatives, even though the big states had most of the population? *(Students may say the small states would never get what they wanted; the big states would always dominate.)*
2. Why do you think the big states didn't want to have the same number of representatives as the little states? *(There were more little states than large states, so the large states would always be outvoted.)*
3. What might be some other ways to balance power among big and small states? *(Responses will vary.)*

WRITE

Suggest that students create a greeting card to thank Roger Sherman for the Great Compromise. As a text for the card, students may wish to write a poem that celebrates Sherman's achievement.

LITERACY LINKS

Words to Discuss

Virginia Plan
New Jersey Plan
Great Compromise

Have students use context to identify the provisions of each plan. *(Virginia Plan—representation decided by population; New Jersey Plan—all states have same number of representatives; Great Compromise—two houses, one based on population, the other with an equal number of representatives from each state)*

Reading Skills
Determining Author's Purpose

Ask students to consider why the author includes the descriptive information about Sherman's age, character, and physical appearance. Ask: What connection do you see between these descriptions and the Great Compromise? *(Help students recognize that the compromise is simple and direct, which fits the various descriptions of Sherman.)*
ANALYZING/SYNTHESIZING

Skills Connection
History/Art

Invite students to compare the verbal descriptions of Roger Sherman with the image painted in the picture on page 173. Have students respond to these questions: Is the artist's image a good reflection of the descriptions people made? Why or why not? What, if anything, did the artist miss? What, if anything, did the verbal descriptions miss?

Just What Is a Constitution?

The Framers intended the Constitution to be the supreme law of the land. Their gift to future generations was a provision for amendment so that the document could change with the times.

ASK

1. Why did opponents of slavery think the Three-Fifths Compromise was a victory? *(Help students see that the compromise prohibited the slave-holding states from counting a slave as a whole person in order to increase the population of the state and, therefore, the number of representatives the state had.)*

2. What is a constitution? *(a basic plan of government that does not include everyday laws)*

3. What are the three branches of government in the United States? *(legislative, judicial, and executive)*

4. On what two basic things did the delegates agree? *(Help students recognize that the delegates agreed on guaranteeing basic human rights and freedoms and on providing a government that exists only by the consent of the governed.)*

5. What is the only way the Constitution can be changed? *(by amendment)*

DISCUSS

1. **Sourcebook:** Have students follow along in the Sourcebook (or on pages 194-198 of the Student Book) as you read aloud the first sentence from each section of Source #20.

2. Have students use Resource 15 (TG page 89) to summarize some of the important provisions of the Constitution.

3. How did the Framers solve the problem of the balance of power in the government? *(They created a government with three branches and a system of checks and balances that enabled each branch to keep the others from becoming too powerful. They also made the Constitution more powerful than the states or any of the branches of government.)*

WRITE

Ask students to assign a grade to the Constitutional Convention for its work and to write a one-paragraph explanation.

Ponder
As the author notes, 10,000 amendments have been proposed to our Constitution, but only 26 have been adopted. Have some great ideas been lost? Is the process of amending the Constitution too strict?

 **Question Chart**

LITERACY LINKS

Words to Discuss

checks and balances ratify
supreme law   amendments
Three-Fifths Compromise

Have students create a word web around the word *constitution*, with sub-webs or branches for each of the words. Suggest that students use context to provide definitions for each term.

Reading Skills
Comparing Texts

Invite students to compare the text of the Constitution (pages 194-199) with that of the English Bill of Rights, found in the Sourcebook (Source #8). What conclusions can they draw about the influence of the English document on the American document? Ask students to share their conclusions with the class. CONNECTING

Skills Connection
History/Mathematics

Challenge students to figure out the number of representatives, senators, and state legislatures that would be required to approve a constitutional amendment today. Suggest that students use an almanac or an Internet search to determine current numbers of representatives and senators if they do not already know them. Then students should use the fractions mentioned in the text to calculate their answers.

Good Words and Bad

The Constitution contains flaws, especially the parts dealing with slavery. But the words *We the People* hold the possibility of perfection, and, through the amendment process, Americans have reached for that ideal.

ASK

1. In which part of the Constitution are the noble aims of the Founders stated? *(the Preamble)*

2. Why did the Founders make compromises in the Constitution? *(so that all the delegates would accept it)*

3. What groups of people are not given citizenship or voting rights in the Constitution? *(women, enslaved people, and Native Americans)*

4. What invention made slavery even more profitable and kept it from ending? *(the cotton gin)*

5. Contrast the words and deeds of John Rutledge, George Mason, and Thomas Jefferson regarding slavery. *(Rutledge spoke in favor of slavery but freed his slaves. Mason and Jefferson spoke against slavery but did not free their slaves.)*

◎ Ponder
The author says "Sometimes it is hard to see things with the eyes of another age." Why is that so difficult?

 **Question Chart**

DISCUSS

1. Why were the Framers unable to find a way to allow Native Americans and settlers to live together? *(Possible response: The Framers represented the settlers, and most settlers wanted land that belonged to the Indians.*

2. How did the issue of slavery force the Framers to compromise between the real and the ideal? *(Possible response: The South refused to give up slavery, and the North had to accept it in order to have all states adopt the Constitution.)*

3. What are some of the paradoxes of history described in this chapter? *(Possible responses: The Founders write "We the people" but left out mention of slaves, women, and Native Americans; the Constitution is a great document, but it includes mistakes; slavery was becoming unprofitable, then the cotton gin revived it; Rutledge spoke in favor of slavery and freed his slaves, but Jefferson and Mason spoke against slavery and did not free their slaves.)*

WRITE

Invite students to write a letter to the Founders regarding the compromises on slavery. Encourage students to propose alternatives that they think might have worked in 1787 and to explain why.

L I T E R A C Y   L I N K S

Words to Discuss

preamble   **cotton gin**
slave trade

Ask students which word is derived from the Latin words for "go before." *(preamble)*

Reading Skills
Previewing

Before students read this chapter, suggest that they scan the chapter title and look at the illustrations and the captions, and then make inferences regarding what the chapter will be about (for example, what the good words and bad words might refer to). Then have students confirm or change their ideas as they read. INFERRING

Meeting Individual Needs
English Language Learners

Students may have difficulty reading the Preamble because it is one long sentence. Help students find the main subject *(We the people)* and verbs *(do ordain and establish)*. Guide students in recognizing that the other phrases make up a list of aims or goals.

No More Secrets

Each delegate had reservations about the Constitution, but few believed any better plan could be devised. They turned the plan over to the states for ratification, which triggered yet another round of conflict and debate.

ASK

1. Why did three delegates leave without signing the Constitution? *(They didn't think it was good enough.)*
2. Why did Washington think the Constitution was a "miracle"? *(because delegates from so many different states had united to form a national government)*
3. What did Patrick Henry dislike about the Constitution? *(He wanted powerful states, not the powerful central government that the Constitution set up.)*
4. What did George Mason think the Constitution should have done? *(end the slave trade)*

DISCUSS

1. Benjamin Franklin found symbolic meaning in two things described in this chapter. What were they? *(a two-headed snake found in a river, and a carving of a half-sun on the chair that George Washington sat in)* What meaning did Franklin see in them? *(He thought the snake was like delegates who were divided over the Constitution, and he said that the sun was rising rather than setting, indicating a new day for the United States after the delegates adopted the new Constitution.)*
2. The delegates signed the Constitution, and it took the states almost another year— until July 1788—to ratify the Constitution. Considering this delay, do you think the delegates were right to hold their meetings in secret? Why or why not? *(Possible responses: They were right because it would have otherwise taken them much longer to create a Constitution. They were wrong because the states should have had more input before the Constitution was finished.)*

WRITE

Invite students to create a script of a dialogue between Benjamin Franklin and Patrick Henry on whether or not to sign the Constitution. Encourage students to use information about each person from previous chapters as well as from the current chapter.

 Ponder
How would you have tried to find out what was going on in the delegates' secret meetings in the summer of 1787? What would you have done with any information you got?

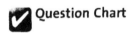 **Question Chart**

L I T E R A C Y   L I N K S

Words to Discuss

ratification

Remind students that they discussed *ratify* in Chapter 39. Have them identify the suffix *-tion* and note the spelling change from *y* to *i* and the addition of *ca*. Students should also notice how the suffix changes the pronunciation by shifting the accented syllable. Have students give similar examples (*modify—modification*; *apply—application*; and so on).

Reading Skills
Reading Between the Lines

Have students review the information about Paul Revere (page 183) and Patrick Henry (page 184). Point out that these men were from two critical states—Massachusetts and Virginia, respectively—in the ratification of the Constitution. Ask the following questions to guide inferences about the vote in these states. Were the voters divided or united about the Constitution? *(divided)* What conclusion

can you draw about the role of Revere and Henry in influencing the vote? *(They were very influential.)* What details support your conclusion? *(The author says Revere "turned the narrow balance" and Henry "almost won.")* INFERRING

If You Can Keep It

As soon as Americans saw the newly written Constitution, they set out to improve it. The price of ratification was a promise to add the ten amendments known today as the Bill of Rights.

ASK

1. What did the state constitutions have that some people thought the Constitution should have? *(bill of rights)*
2. Who wrote the Bill of Rights for the Constitution? *(James Madison)*
3. Which of the first ten amendments is the most important? *(the first)* What does it guarantee? *(basic freedoms—religion, speech, press, assembly, and petition)*
4. What two things convinced North Carolina to ratify the Constitution? *(George Washington agreeing to be president and the Bill of Rights)*

 Ponder
What does it take to "keep a republic" as Franklin said? What can you do to help?

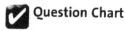 **Question Chart**

DISCUSS

1. **Sourcebook:** Read aloud from Source #20 and have students follow along in their Sourcebook or on Student Book page 199. Have students paraphrase the basic idea of each of the first ten amendments.
2. What did the Federalists and the anti-Federalists disagree about? *(The Federalists liked the Constitution. They liked federalism, which was a balance between the national government and state governments. The anti-Federalists wanted stronger states' rights. They did not want a strong national government.)*
3. How did Alexander Hamilton and Patrick Henry show what is meant by the "American way"? *(Neither person got exactly what he wanted in the Constitution, but when it was ratified, each supported it and encouraged others to do so. They didn't hold a grudge.)*

WRITE

Ask students to write a letter to the editor in response to the statements made by Europeans (page 188) regarding the new nation.

L I T E R A C Y   L I N K S

Words to Discuss

Bill of Rights
republic
anti-federalist

Have students brainstorm some of the multiple meanings of *bill* and identify which one fits the term Bill of Rights. *(a written document)*

Reading Skills
Analyzing Rhetorical Devices

Remind students that the author often directs questions to readers and uses the word *you* to address readers. Ask students to write a few sentences expressing their views on this practice. Then have students read the last paragraph of the chapter. Have the class discuss how these words affect them. ANALYZING

Meeting Individual Needs
English Language Learners

To help students grasp information about the Bill of Rights, have them work with more-fluent partners to create a graphic organizer listing the amendment numbers and summarizing the content or aim of each amendment.

THINKING ABOUT THE THEMES

The following questions will help students relate the book's themes to the content of Part 7. You may wish to use these questions for classroom discussion or have students answer them in written form.

1. What were some of the conflicts over power that the delegates faced in 1787? *(Guide students in summarizing conflicts that included how the states would be represented in the national legislature; how the power of the states would be balanced against the power of the national government; how to deal with slavery; and how power would be balanced among the branches of the national government.)*

2. Compromise is one way to resolve conflict. How did the Great Compromise resolve a conflict? *(It set up two houses in the national legislature, the House of Representatives and the Senate. In the House, representation is based on each state's population; in the Senate, representation is the same for all states.)*

3. Do you think the delegates successfully resolved the conflict over slavery in 1787? Why or why not? *(Help students explain that most anti-slavery delegates compromised in order to get the Constitution ratified. Delegates from slave-holding states also compromised by agreeing to the Three-Fifths clause of the Constitution. These compromises did not resolve the conflict so much as postpone it. Conflicts over slavery continued for many more years.)*

4. How did the country change after ratifying the Constitution? *(Guide students in summarizing that the country changed from a group of independent states to a federal republic in which the Constitution is the supreme law of the land.)*

5. Draw students' attention to the themes that have been posted around the room. Give them the opportunity to explore the relevance of these themes to to Part 7. Accept choices that are supported by sound reasoning.

ASSESSING PART 7

Use Check-Up 7 (TG page 74) to assess student learning.

PROJECTS AND ACTIVITIES

▶ Hamilton to Hamilton

Invite student pairs to imagine that one of them is Andrew Hamilton of Pennsylvania, defender of Peter Zenger, and the other is Alexander Hamilton of New York after the Bill of Rights has been ratified. Ask students to discuss the changes that have taken place over time and why those changes have taken place. Students should focus on the political climate in which the first Hamilton defended the rights of a colonist against English rule versus a time in which independent Americans made their own rules for their future.

▶ To Sign or Not to Sign

Ask students to imagine that they are delegates to the Constitutional Convention who oppose slavery. Would they, like George Mason, refuse to sign the Constitution? Or would they, like Ben Franklin, place their faith in the amendment process? To encourage discussion, have students weigh some of the possible outcomes of each decision.

▶ Pulling Jefferson's Coattail

Read aloud the following selection from a letter in which Benjamin Banneker challenges Thomas Jefferson to reexamine his position on slavery.

> Sir, suffer me to recall to your mind that time in which . . . the tyranny of the British crown . . . reduced you to a state of servitude.

Ask students to complete the letter, presenting arguments in favor of amending the Constitution to abolish slavery.

★★ **FACTS TO SHARE** ★★

The bald eagle was initially chosen as the national emblem in 1782 and became the official symbol in 1787. The eagle was chosen because it has a long life, great strength, and a majestic appearance. Its long wingspan and swooping flight makes it seem the very essence of freedom. Ben Franklin, however, objected to the choice. He thought the bald eagle "a bird of bad moral character . . . and a rank coward." He favored the wild turkey, which he found "a much more respectable bird . . . and a bird of courage."

Name _____ Date _____

Check-Up 1

Answering these questions will help you understand and remember what you have read in Chapters 1-6. Write your answers on a separate sheet of paper.

1. The following individuals played key roles in the events described in Chapters 1-6. What did each person do that was important?
   a. Peter Zenger
   b. Andrew Hamilton
   c. William Johnson

2. Explain who fought on opposing sides in the French and Indian War. How were the Indians an important factor in the war?

3. Define each of these terms. Then tell why the term was important in the time.
   a. libel
   b. Iroquois League
   c. mission

4. What did Benjamin Franklin think the colonists should learn from the Iroquois?

5. Compare the Albany Congress with the meeting of William Johnson and the Iroquois at Johnson's home. Which was more successful? Why?

6. In the first half of the French and Indian War, the British lost most of the important battles. In the second half, they won all the important battles. What caused this change?

7. What effect did the end of the war and the Treaty of Paris have on each of these groups living in North America?
   a. French colonists in Acadia
   b. Native Americans
   c. Spanish colonists

8. Choose one person from this period whom you admire. Describe what you admire about the person, and why. Taking no more than five minutes, draw a quick portrait of this person.

9. Following are two major conflicts in this period. Choose one and describe the changes that occurred because of the conflict.
   a. authority of the royal governor versus colonists' right to criticize government officials
   b. English territorial claims versus French territorial claims

10. Complete the cause-effect chart about the French and Indian War. The first one has been done for you.

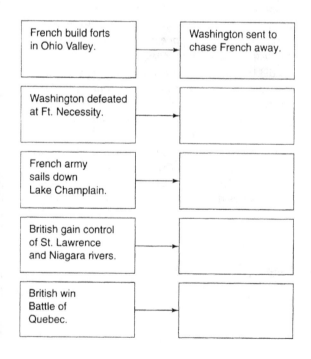

Name _____   Date _____

Check-Up 2

Answering these questions will help you understand and remember what you have read in Chapters 7-10. Write your answers on a separate sheet of paper.

1. These people played key roles in events described in Chapters 7-10. What did each person do that was important?
   a. Sir William Johnson
   b. Hector St. John Crèvecoeur
   c. Eliza Lucas Pinckney

2. Geography was important to the colonists. Tell what impact each of these geographical features had on colonists' westward movement after the French and Indian War.
   a. Appalachian Mountains
   b. Ohio River valley
   c. Cumberland Gap

3. Define each of these terms. Then tell why the term was important to the events of the time.
   a. Proclamation of 1763
   b. yeoman farmers
   c. habeas corpus

4. Explain how Hector St. John Crèvecoeur thought that colonial Americans were different from people in Europe.

5. Imagine that you are a reporter from England who has just interviewed Eliza Lucas Pinckney. You learned about her life and interests. Make notes for your article about this independent-minded American.

6. How did each of the following help English people gain rights?
   a. Magna Carta
   b. Glorious Revolution

7. Imagine that you are living on the frontier west of the Appalachian Mountains. Write a letter to someone on the East Coast. Tell the person how you feel about making your own rules and taking care of yourself.

8. What changes made the colonists more independent? How did these changes lead to conflict with England?

9. How is Eliza Pinckney an example of Crèvecoeur's "new American"?

10. How might colonists have crossed the Appalachian Mountain to settle in the Ohio Valley and Kentucky?

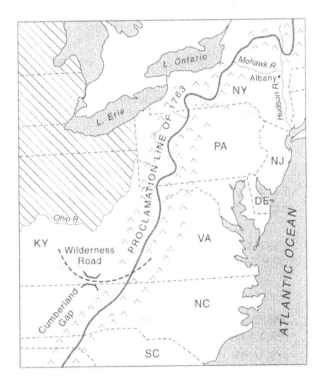

Name _____   Date _____

Check-Up 3

Answering these questions will help you understand and remember what you have read in Chapters 11-15. Write your answers on a separate sheet of paper.

1. These groups of people played key roles in events described in Chapters 11-15. Tell how the people in each group are connected and what each person did that was important in this period.
   a. Samuel Adams, Thomas Paine, Patrick Henry
   b. Paul Revere, William Dawes, Samuel Prescott, Captain John Parker
   c. Ethan Allen, Benedict Arnold

2. Name the city or colony where each of these events occurred. Then tell what happened.
   a. massacre
   b. tea party
   c. battles between British troops and minutemen

3. Define each of these terms. Then tell why it is important to the time.
   a. Committees of Correspondence
   b. Quartering Act
   c. Continental Congress

4. What taxes did the British government place on the American colonists? How did the colonists react to those taxes?

5. How did the difficulties in transportation affect communication between the American colonies?

6. Describe a trip by stagecoach from Boston to New York. Explain how long it took, the conditions of the road, and what the traveler would experience.

7. How would the Boston Massacre be viewed by a British soldier stationed in Boston? by a resident of Boston? Write a paragraph contrasting these two points of view.

8. Imagine that you are at Concord in early April 1775. You see the colonists gathering cannons and gunpowder. Write two or three diary entries that tell what happened from that time until "the shot heard round the world" on April 19, 1775. Include what Patriot leaders and minutemen are doing, and rumors you hear about what the British are doing.

9. Following are two major conflicts in this period. Choose one and describe the results of the conflict.
   a. British government versus colonists over taxes
   b. British government versus colonists over quartering soldiers

10. Indicate the year of these important events leading up to the American Revolution on the timeline. Label the timeline with the corresponding letters.
   a. Boston Tea Party
   b. Stamp Tax Congress
   c. Boston Massacre
   d. Battles of Lexington and Concord
   e. First Continental Congress

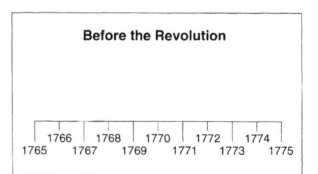

Before the Revolution

| 1765 | 1766 | 1767 | 1768 | 1769 | 1770 | 1771 | 1772 | 1773 | 1774 | 1775 |

Name _____ Date _____

Check-Up 4

Answering these questions will help you understand and remember what you have read in Chapters 16-21. Write your answers on a separate sheet of paper.

1. What did each of these delegates do that was especially important at the Second Continental Congress?
   a. George Washington
   b. Thomas Jefferson
   c. John Hancock
   d. John Adams
   e. Benjamin Franklin

2. Choose two other delegates to the Second Continental Congress. Tell something about their beliefs and qualifications as delegates.

3. The geography of the Boston area was important in the Battle of Bunker Hill. Identify each of these places. Then tell the role each played in the battle.
   a. Charles River
   b. Charlestown
   c. Breed's Hill

4. Geography also played a role at the Battle of Charleston. Tell how each of the following was important in that battle.
   a. Charleston Harbor
   b. Sullivan's Island
   c. shoals
   d. palmetto trees

5. Define each of these terms. Then tell why the term was important in the time.
   a. militia
   b. congress
   c. Olive Branch Petition
   d. consent of the governed

6. The Second Continental Congress met in May 1776. War had not yet been declared. Why did the Congress think it was necessary to prepare for war?

7. Imagine you are a delegate to the Continental Congress. Write a letter to one of your relatives back home. Tell what the Congress is doing and how you feel about it.

8. In a declaration, a writer states something in a stirring manner. In the Declaration of Independence, what did Thomas Jefferson state about these topics?
   a. independence
   b. King George III
   c. equality
   d. rights
   e. consent of the governed

9. What effect did the Battle of Bunker Hill have on the Americans?

10. Although the British soldiers were the best in the world, their generals made terrible mistakes at Bunker Hill and Charleston. In the chart, write a conclusion about why the generals made each mistake. One has been done for you.

Bunker Hill	Conclusion
Soldiers had to fight entrenched Americans.	Generals thought Americans were lazy. Didn't notice them digging trenches.
Soldiers had to charge uphill under heavy fire.	

Charleston	Conclusion
Ships ran aground; soldiers could not wade ashore.	
Cannonballs stuck in side of Fort Sullivan.	

Name _____ Date _____

Check-Up 5

Answering these questions will help you understand and remember what you have read in Chapters 22-28. Write your answers on a separate sheet of paper.

1. Imagine the people in each pair are talking to each other. Write a few sentences that each person would say. The sentences should introduce the person and tell what he or she did in the American Revolution.
   a. Molly Pitcher, Molly Brant
   b. Martha Washington, Abigail Adams
   c. Marquis de Lafayette, Baron von Steuben
   d. General John Burgoyne, General Horatio Gates

2. Suppose you are drawing a map of the American Revolution. Why would you show these places on your map? Explain why each is important.
   a. New York City
   b. Saratoga, New York
   c. Valley Forge, Pennsylvania
   d. Ohio Valley

3. Choose someone from this period whom you think is a hero. Explain why you chose the person.

4. Write a paragraph explaining why the author describes the American Revolution as a "people's war." Use these points in your explanation: women, children, and slaves fought; citizens became soldiers; the spirit of Valley Forge.

5. Imagine that you could interview James Forten. Write how he would answer each of these questions.
   a. Why did you want to fight for the Patriots?
   b. What did you do during the war?
   c. Why and how did you remain an American?

6. Explain how both of these people helped the American cause during the Revolution: Marquis de Lafayette, Haym Salomon.

7. You are a British soldier with General Burgoyne. Tell how the general's plans to capture the Hudson River valley and split the colonies backfired.

8. How was George Washington a great leader on and off the battlefield?

9. The Battle of Saratoga is often called the turning point of the American Revolution. What changed as a result of that battle?

10. People from all over North America and Europe fought or worked for the Patriot cause. Copy the chart on a separate sheet of paper. Complete it with details about each of the people listed. Then write a sentence expressing what they had in common.

Person	Country	Background	Why Fought
Marquis de Lafayette			
James Forten			
Thaddeus Kosciuszko			
Haym Salomon			

Name _____   Date _____

Check-Up 6

Answering these questions will help you understand and remember what you have read in Chapters 29-34. Write your answers on a separate sheet of paper.

1. These people played key roles in the Battle of Yorktown. Tell who each person was and what he did in the battle. For pairs or groups of names, explain how the persons are connected to one another.
   a. Lord Charles Cornwallis, General Henry Clinton
   b. Admiral de Grasse
   c. Comte de Rochambeau, George Washington
   d. Marquis de Lafayette, Baron von Steuben, General Anthony Wayne

2. In the late 1700s big changes were taking place west of the Appalachians. Tell what was happening in each group of present-day states.
   a. California, New Mexico, Arizona, Texas
   b. Ohio, Illinois, Indiana, Michigan, Wisconsin, Minnesota

3. Two "separations" were part of the plan for the new nation. Explain the meaning of each of these terms and how it relates to the new government.
   a. separation of powers
   b. separation of church and state

4. Who was Mary Katherine Goddard? Tell what these four terms have to do with her life:
   a. Declaration of Independence
   b. protecting sources of information
   c. women's rights
   d. slavery

5. The Articles of Confederation gave most power to the states. They gave almost no power to the national government. Tell what problem this caused in each of these areas.
   a. voting power of large and small states
   b. government's power to tax
   c. building an army
   d. citizens' sense of loyalty

6. Why does the author call the Northwest Ordinance a "first" in world history?

7. Answer the following questions about the Northwest Ordinance.
   a. What states gave up land that became part of the Northwest Territory?
   b. What states were eventually created from the territory?
   c. What were some of the guarantees made to settlers?

8. Imagine that you want people to vote for Thomas Jefferson as Person of the Year. Write a paragraph telling why you think he deserves the award.

9. After the Revolutionary War, there were still plenty of conflicts in America. Choose one of these conflicts. Describe the conflict and the change that resulted from it.
   a. states versus states
   b. Native Americans versus settlers
   c. Virginia state government versus freedom of religion

10. This map shows the six states that were created completely or partially from the Northwest Territory. Using the map on pages 212-213 in your textbook, identify and label each of the states on this map.

Name _____   Date _____

Check-Up 7

Answering these questions will help you understand and remember what you have read in Chapters 35-42. Write your answers on a separate sheet of paper.

1. James Madison is called the "Father of the Constitution." List at least three reasons why he deserves this title.

2. Choose two other delegates to the Constitutional Convention. What was their background? Describe their beliefs about the best government for the new nation.

3. Define each term. Then explain how it was important in the new government.
   a. confederation
   b. federation
   c. legislature
   d. executive
   e. judiciary
   f. houses
   g. amendment
   h. ratify

4. Imagine that you are writing a paragraph explaining our government to someone from another country. Use these three ideas in your explanation.
   a. unalienable rights
   b. consent of the governed
   c. checks and balances

5. How was the Virginia Plan different from the New Jersey Plan?

6. How did the Great Compromise save the Constitution?

7. Slavery was a hot topic at the Convention. Describe the arguments each of the following Framers would have made.
   a. one who wanted to outlaw slavery
   b. one who wanted to keep slavery
   c. one who believed compromise was necessary

8. Explain why George Mason and Patrick Henry disliked the Constitution.

9. The Constitution changed the government from a confederation of equal states to a federal system. What compromises made this change possible?

10. On a separate sheet of paper, copy the web. Then fill in what each of the people named might say about the meaning of *We the people.*

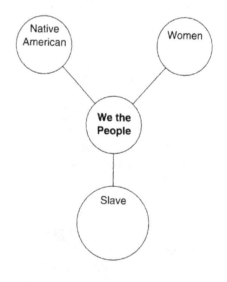

Name _____ Date _____

Resource 1

QUESTION CHART: *FROM COLONIES TO COUNTRY*

★ What were the major events?

_____   _____
_____   _____
_____   _____
_____   _____
_____   _____

★ Who were the significant people?

_____   _____
_____   _____
_____   _____
_____   _____
_____   _____

★ What were the important ideas?

_____
_____
_____
_____
_____

Name _____ Date _____

Resource 2

EUROPEAN COLONIAL CLAIMS IN NORTH AMERICA

Directions   Fill in the outline map below, using information you have learned about how Britain, France, and Spain battled for territory in North America.

1. Using three different-colored pencils, fill in the areas claimed by each European nation about 1750. Complete the map legend showing the color for each nation.

2. By 1763, France had lost its territory in North America. Draw hatch marks (diagonal lines) showing this territory. For land that went to Spain, draw the lines from upper left to lower right. For land that went to England, draw the lines from upper right to lower left.

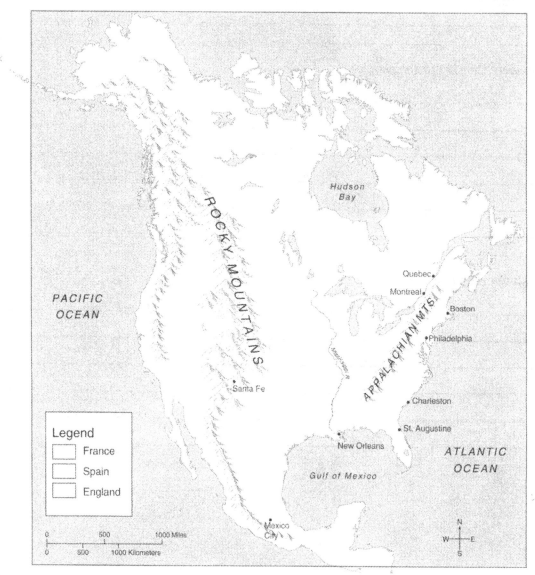

Resource 3

A MOTHER'S CHILDREN

Directions   **Read this poem written by Benjamin Franklin in 1763. Then answer the questions.**

Know ye, bad neighbors, with aim to divide
The sons from the mother, that she's still our pride,
And if you attack her, we're all on her side,
Which nobody can deny, deny.

1. What does Franklin think of the ties between the colonists and England in 1763? What clues does he give that indicate his thinking?

_____

_____

_____

2. Predict how those ties might change. Use any hints you have discovered in Chapters 1-6 about what the colonists want and what Britain wants.

_____

_____

_____

3. Write your own poem about an event or person in Chapters 1-6. Express an opinion about the event or person. Include details and clues that help readers understand what you're describing and what you think about it.

_____

_____

_____

_____

_____

_____

_____

_____

_____

Name _____ Date _____

Resource 4

STACKING UP THE COLONIES

Numerical information about a topic can be expressed using visual aids. Two of those visual aids are a *table* and a *bar graph*. A **table** presents exact numbers about a topic in an orderly fashion. A **bar graph** turns those numbers into a dramatic visual aid that makes it easy for the reader to understand the importance of the numbers.

Directions Use the population figures in the table to make a horizontal bar graph. Order the colonies from largest at the top to smallest at the bottom. (The bars for Virginia and Massachusetts have been done.) Follow these steps.

1. Using a ruler and a pencil, mark the length of the bar for each state.
2. Using the ruler and pencil, draw the bars.
3. Use a different-colored pencil or crayon to fill in each bar.

Virginia	447,000	Connecticut	184,000	New Hampshire	62,000
Massachusetts	267,000	New York	163,000	Rhode Island	58,000
Pennsylvania	240,000	South Carolina	124,000	Delaware	36,000
Maryland	203,000	New Jersey	117,000	Georgia	24,000
North Carolina	197,000				

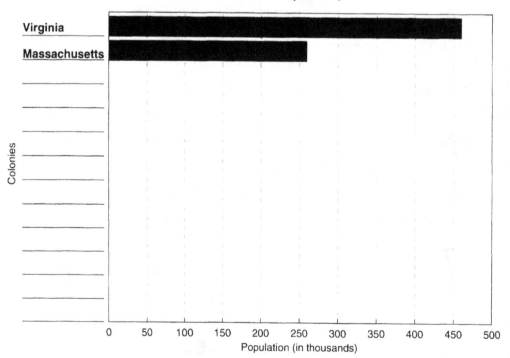

Colonial Population, 1770

Name _____ Date _____

Resource 5

A HARD LIFE FOR SLAVES

To research the past, historians use primary sources and secondary sources. A **primary source** is something said or written by a person who was alive at the time of the events. A **secondary source** is written or recorded by people using primary sources long after the events took place. Letters, diaries, and official documents are kinds of primary sources. Encyclopedias and textbooks are kinds of secondary sources.

Directions   **Read these accounts of the treatment of slaves. One is from a primary source. The others are from secondary sources. Then answer the questions.**

Field hands worked longer than any other kind of slave. Their workday generally lasted from sunrise to sunset. Some field hands were housed as well as free workers. But many others lived under the worst conditions.—*World Book Encyclopedia*

[H]ousing was seldom good; slaves usually lived in small one- or two-room cabins, windowless and unfloored. . . . The diet almost always included pork (fatback), meal, molasses, and whatever vegetables the slaves could raise themselves. . . . —*Encyclopedia of Black America*

The principal food of those upon my master's plantation consisted of corn-meal and salt herrings [fish]; to which was added in summer a little buttermilk, and the few vegetables which each might raise for himself and his family. . . .
   In ordinary times, we had two regular meals a day: breakfast at twelve o'clock, after laboring from daylight, and supper when the work of . . . the day was over. . . . Our dress was of tow cloth; for children, nothing but a shirt. . . .
   We lodged in log huts, and on the bare ground. Wooden floors were an unknown luxury. In a single room were huddled, like cattle, ten or a dozen persons, men, women, and children. . . . Our beds were collections of straw and old rags, thrown down in the corners and boxed in with boards. . . . The wind whistled and the rain and snow blew through the cracks, and the damp earth soaked in the moisture till the floor was [muddy] as a pig-sty.—*Josiah Henson*

1. What are the names of the secondary sources? Who wrote the primary source?

_____

_____

2. What clues in the text tell you the third document is a primary source?

_____

_____

3. What do you think are the advantages of using a primary source in researching history? What are the advantages of using secondary sources?

_____

_____

Name _____ Date _____

Resource 6

COMPARING FIREBRANDS

Directions   Complete the chart to create a brief profile of each Firebrand. Then answer the questions.

	Samuel Adams	Thomas Paine	Patrick Henry
How did he make himself heard?			
What failure(s) did he have early in his life?			
Where did he live?			
Describe two important things he said or did.			

1. What idea did all the Firebrands agree about?

_____

2. Which Firebrand would you most like to meet? Tell why.

_____

_____

Name _____ Date _____

Resource 7

FOLLOWING THE KING'S HIGHWAY

Directions   The major colonial route between Boston and New York City was the Boston Post Road. In time, it became part of a road network called the King's Highway. Study the map and then answer the questions.

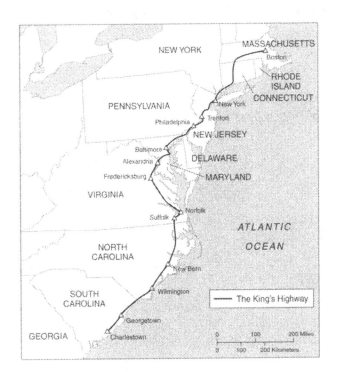

1. Use the map scale to figure out the approximate length of the King's Highway.

_____

2. Through which colonies did the King's Highway pass?

_____

_____

3. If you traveled by wagon, you could cover 20-25 miles a day. If your wagon traveled 20 miles a day, how long would it take you to go from New York City to Philadelphia?

_____

4. If your wagon traveled 25 miles a day, how long would it take you to travel the entire distance from Boston to Charlestown?

_____

Name _____ Date _____

Resource 8

DELEGATE CROSSWORD

Directions   Use the clues to fill in the crossword puzzle with the last names of delegates to the Second Continental Congress.

Then, on a separate sheet of paper, create your own crossword puzzle using the names of delegates. Write clues for solving the puzzle. (Use different clues if you are using the names of delegates in the puzzle below.)

Across
3. Thirty-three-year-old cousin of Peyton Randolph
7. Believed slavery should be ended by law

Down
1. Helped organize first Committee of Correspondence
2. Tried to get Canadians to join the revolution
4. Elected governor of Rhode Island 10 times
5. Set up first free clinic in America
6. Shouted "It's done! And I will abide by it."

Name _____ Date _____

Resource 9

THE BATTLE OF BUNKER HILL

Directions Reread the account in your textbook of the Battle of Bunker Hill (Chapter 18). Pay special attention to the illustration on pages 90-91. Use the information in your textbook and on the map below to complete the activity.

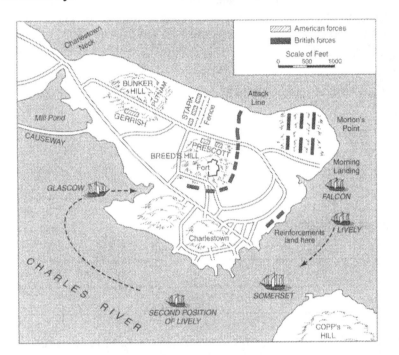

1. What can you tell from the map about the number of British forces versus the number of American forces?

_____

2. Use the map scale to figure out the distance from Charlestown to Charlestown Neck.

_____

3. On the map, draw a dotted line showing how the British might have captured Charlestown Neck. Then tell why it was lucky for the Americans that they didn't.

_____

_____

_____

Resource 10

WHOSE RIGHTS?

Directions   **Read what John Adams wrote in 1776. Then answer the questions.**

> There will be no end to it [talk of independence]. New claims will arise; women will demand a vote; lads from twelve to twenty-one will not think their rights enough attended to, and every man who has not a farthing [quarter of a penny], will demand an equal voice with any other, in all acts of state.

1. What does Adams's opinion of independence seem to be? Use examples from the passage to support your opinion.

_____

_____

_____

2. Do you think Adams was correct? Why or why not?

_____

_____

_____

3. Imagine you are Abigail Adams or Benjamin Banneker. Write a letter to a relative in which you give your opinion about the Declaration of Independence.

_____

_____

_____

_____

_____

_____

_____

_____

_____

_____

Name _____ Date _____

Resource 11

THE WAR NUMBERS

Directions   **Review the information about the Revolution in the chart. Then use the information to answer the questions.**

Population of American Colonies	1770	2,148,100
	1780	2,780,400
Americans Enrolled in Military		200,000
Americans Killed in Combat	Army	4,049
	Navy	342
	Marines	49
Americans Wounded in Combat	Army	6,004
	Navy	114
	Marines	70
Cost of War (in today's dollars)		$1,200,000,000

1. How much did the population of the colonies increase between 1770 and 1780?

_____

2. What is the total number of Americans killed during the Revolution?

_____

3. What is the total number of Americans wounded during the Revolution?

_____

4. How many American soldiers survived the war without being killed or wounded?

_____

5. The war lasted for eight years. What was the average cost per year?

_____

Resource 12

TURNING POINTS OF THE WAR

Directions Below are important events in the American Revolution. Match each one with the letter of the appropriate effect. Write the letter of the effect on the line by the event. Then answer the question.

EVENT

_____ **1.** Lexington and Concord

_____ **2.** Bunker Hill

_____ **3.** Long Island

_____ **4.** Trenton and Princeton

_____ **5.** Saratoga

_____ **6.** Valley Forge

EFFECT

a. Americans prove they can stand up to the British in regular battle.

b. American victory convinces France to join the war against Britain.

c. Surprise victories raise American morale at lowest point of war.

d. American army survives winter and comes out a well-trained unit.

e. Massachusetts militia force British to retreat.

f. Washington keeps army in the field despite overwhelming British victories.

7. Which of these turning points do you think was most important? Explain.

_____

_____

_____

Name _____ Date _____

Resource 13

BATTLING IT OUT AT YORKTOWN

Directions   The map shows the Battle of Yorktown. Use information from the map and from Chapter 31 to answer the questions.

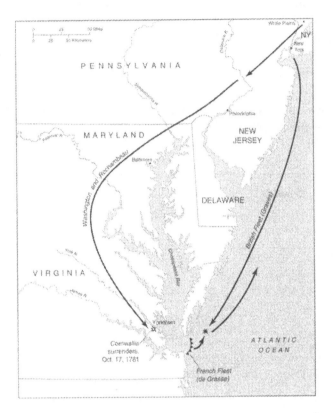

1. On the map, what two rivers is Yorktown between? What other large body of water is nearby?

_____

2. Why did Cornwallis choose this location near water for his base?

_____

3. Use the map scale at the top of the map. Estimate how far Washington's troops had to march to get from White Plains to Yorktown. It took them about 40 days. About how many miles did they travel each day?

_____

4. Why did Yorktown turn into a trap for Cornwallis?

_____

Name _____ Date _____

Resource 14

THOMAS JEFFERSON'S WEB SITE

Directions   **Complete this Web site for Thomas Jefferson. Follow these steps.**

1. **Memorial page:** Post the three things Jefferson wanted to be remembered for.

2. **Achievements page:** Post other things Jefferson did in his life.

3. **Contact TJ page:** Post some comments about Jefferson by friends and critics.

4. **Home page:** Copy or draw a picture of Jefferson or of something that you feel represents Jefferson. Finally, write the name of the site on the line.

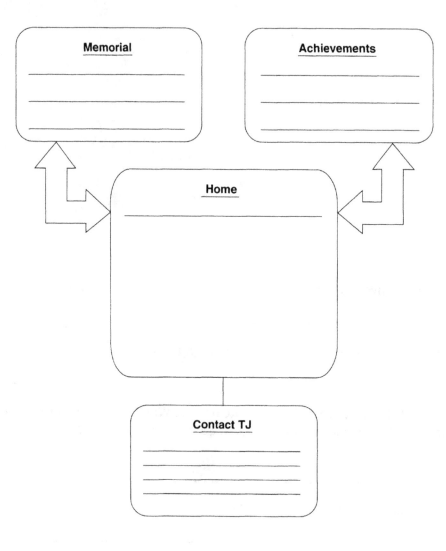

Name _____ Date _____

Resource 15

WHERE DOES THE CONSTITUTION SAY THAT?

Directions   Part I sends you on a search through the Constitution (pages 194-199). When you find the information the questions ask for, write the Article and Section numbers in the blanks. (Some Articles do not have Sections.)

   Part II asks you about the balance of power between states and the nation (page 176). Write *state* or *national* in the blanks to tell which level of government has authority over each activity.

Part I

1. How many representatives are there?
   Article _____ Section _____

2. What is the Senate?
   Article _____ Section _____

3. Which branch has the power to tax?
   Article _____ Section _____

4. Who can be President?
   Article _____ Section _____

5. What military and civil powers does the President have?
   Article _____ Section _____

6. What cases does the Supreme Court hear
   Article _____ Section _____

7. How shall new states enter the Union?
   Article _____ Section _____

8. What amendments are forbidden?
   Article _____ Section _____

9. What law is supreme in the nation?
   Article _____ Section _____

10. How was the Constitution to be ratified?
    Article _____ Section _____

Part II

1. schools _____

2. post office _____

3. business between states _____

4. foreign affairs _____

5. local government _____

6. roads _____

ANSWER KEY

CHECK-UP 1

1. (a) New York newspaper publisher who criticized royal governor and was accused of libel (b) most famous lawyer in the colonies who successfully defended Zenger (c) colonial with close ties to the Native Americans

2. Opponents were the British, their colonists, and their Indian allies (Iroquois) versus the French, their colonists, and their Indian allies. The Indians supplied many warriors, and the Iroquois alliance with the British tipped the balance of the war. The Indians also taught the Europeans the frontier style of fighting.

3. (a) Printing something known to be untrue about someone; Zenger's trial for libel established freedom of speech and of the press in the colonies. (b) Confederation of six Native American tribes; it gave Ben Franklin the idea for uniting the colonies. (c) Spanish settlement, built around a church and a fort; the Spanish spread their influence by building missions in California and the Southwest.

4. Franklin believed the colonists should follow the example of the Iroquois League and unite to strengthen themselves and stop conflicts between them.

5. Both tried to get the Iroquois to ally with the British. The Congress was unsuccessful, whereas Johnson, with his personal relationship with the Iroquois, was successful. The Congress also tried to get the colonies to unite, but failed at this because the colonies distrusted each other.

6. In the first battles, the British underestimated the French, were poorly prepared for frontier warfare, and had inexperienced military leaders. In the later battles, they used larger forces, made better use of their navy, had the Iroquois as their allies, and had better generals.

7. (a) Most were moved from Acadia to British colonies or Louisiana. (b) Native Americans were thanked and then abandoned by the British. (c) Spain gained all the western land that had belonged to France, but lost Florida to the British.

8. Responses will vary. Accept either illustrations or verbal portraits.

9. (a) The Zenger trial established freedom of the press and freedom of speech. (b) The French were kicked out of North America, leaving the British and Spanish in control.

10. French build forts in Ohio Valley; Washington sent to chase French away. Washington defeated at Ft. Necessity; Braddock sent to attack Ft. Duquesne. French army sails down Lake Champlain; British and Indians under Warraghiyagey defeat French at Battle of Lake George. British gain control of St. Lawrence and Niagara rivers; French are cut off from supplies and reinforcements. British win Battle of Quebec; French surrender Canada.

CHECK-UP 2

1. (a) colonial leader who signed a treaty that gave Indians money for land the settlers wanted west of the

Appalachians (b) Frenchman who settled in the colonies and described Americans and American society. (c) skilled, hard-working plantation owner who began South Carolina's indigo trade

2. (a) Because of their height and ruggedness, they blocked westward travel. (b) Area of good farmland west of the Appalachians that attracted many colonial settlers. (c) Break in the Appalachians that settlers could use to get to Kentucky.

3. (a) British Parliament's ban on settlement on Indian lands west of the Appalachians; colonists refused to obey it, causing conflict with Indians and British. (b). People who owned their own small farms; made America different from Europe, where aristocrats owned most of the land. (c). An English right that says you can't be arrested without cause; Americans thought they should have this right.

4. Crèvecoeur believed Americans had different ideas about being free, independent, and tolerant of others.

5. Notes should include Pinckney's education, business ability, interest in many subjects, and dedication and hard work.

6. (a) curbed the power of the British king (b) gave British people a Bill of Rights; made the people more powerful than the monarchs

7. Responses will vary.

8. The colonists began to move west, they were far from Britain, they included people from different backgrounds, they were able to take care of themselves. When the British tried to control the colonists, the colonists became angry and resisted.

9. She had her own ideas about marriage; as a woman, she did things that she might not have been allowed to do in England; she was fair and kind to other people.

10. They could use the Mohawk River to get to the Great Lakes; use the Cumberland Gap to get to Kentucky.

CHECK-UP 3

1. (a) All three were firebrands of the American Revolution: Adams created trouble with the British, Paine wrote *Common Sense* which explained why the colonists wanted to separate from Great Britain, and Henry gave fiery speeches that stirred up anger against the British. (b) All played a role in the battles of Lexington and Concord: Revere, Dawes, and Prescott rode out to warn the colonists, and Parker was in charge of the minutemen. (c) Together, they captured the British Fort Ticonderoga; Allen led the Green Mountain Boys, and Arnold fought there as a colonel in the Continental army.

2. (a) Boston; English troops fired on mob of American colonists, causing much anger in the colonies. (b) Boston; colonists dumped British tea into Boston Harbor to protest a tax on tea; British closed Boston Harbor, making colonists think about independence. (c) Massachusetts; English troops tried to capture colonial military stockpiles and leaders, but minutemen fought back and made them retreat.

3. (a) Colonial leaders who wrote letters to each other to try to solve problems in the colonies; they united the colonies in opposition to British. (b) British law that said British soldiers could stay in colonists' homes; it made the colonists even angrier. (c) Meeting of colonial leaders; they discussed mutual problems and what to do about them.

4. The British placed taxes on printed paper, lead, glass, paper, paint, and tea. These made the colonists angry with British rule, because they felt that, since they were not represented in Parliament, Parliament did not have a right to tax them.

5. The roads between cities were very bad, and became worse in bad weather, so travel and mail delivery took a long time. Sea travel was not fast, either, so contact between colonies was poor.

6. Possible response: It's the worst trip I've ever had in my life. It's like trying to ride a wild horse for eighteen hours a day. My bones feel as though they're going to break and I'm feeling sick to my stomach. We stop for just three or four hours at night and I have to sleep with my clothes on.

7. Possible response: a British soldier might believe his life was threatened, a colonist might believe that British soldiers should not be in Boston anyway.

8. Responses will vary, but should include details about the colonists collecting military stores and talking against the British, the British marching out from Boston, the warning rides of Revere, Dawes, and Prescott, the gathering of the minutemen, and the battles.

9. (a) The colonists protested against British taxes; most were repealed but they inflamed anti-British opinion. (b) The colonists didn't want to quarter British troops; resentment over this led to the Boston Massacre.

10. (a) 1773 (b) 1765 (c) 1770 (d) 1775 (e) 1774

CHECK-UP 4

1. (a) became commander of the Continental army (b) wrote Declaration of Independence (c) became President of the Congress (d) nominated Washington as army commander, talked Jefferson into writing the Declaration, did more than anyone to get the Declaration signed (e) served on committee that wrote the Declaration

2. Responses will vary.

3. (a) Separates Boston from Charlestown, where American forces had dug fortifications. British sent troops by boat to attack the Americans. (b) town on the Charlestown peninsula where American forces gathered (c) hill above Charlestown that American forces fortified and tried to defend against British attack

4. (a) British ships tried to sail into it to attack Charleston. (b) island on which Fort Sullivan stood, which British needed to capture. (c) sandbars in Charleston Harbor on which British ships ran aground (d) Trees used for walls of Fort Sullivan; they absorbed British cannon fire, causing the attack to fail.

5. (a) A group of armed citizen soldiers; Washington had to make an army out of these untrained citizens. (b) Elected

leaders who meet to discuss issues; at their meeting, the leaders took action to try to solve problems. (c) Statement colonists sent to Britain; it was colonists' last attempt to solve problems with Britain peacefully. (d) Rule agreed to by those being ruled; this was the kind of government the colonists wanted, as stated in the Declaration.

6. After the battles at Lexington and Concord, it seemed that there was no way to avoid war with Britain. So, although they still tried to come to a peaceful agreement with the British, they knew they had to prepare for war.

7. Responses will vary. Letters should mention naming a general, forming an army, and writing a declaration. Writers might express worry or resolve.

8. (a) The colonies must separate from Britain. (b) The king was not giving the colonists' their rights. (c) All men are created equal. (d) Citizens have rights that their government can never take away. (e) People who are governed must agree to the rules of their government.

9. Although the British finally took the hills, the Americans learned that they could stand up to the British army.

10. Bunker Hill: Soldiers had to fight entrenched Americans./Generals thought Americans were lazy; didn't notice them digging trenches. Soldiers had to charge uphill under heavy fire./Generals didn't think about trying to trap Americans. Charleston: Ships ran aground; soldiers could not wade ashore./Generals had poor information about harbor. Cannonballs stuck in side of Fort Sullivan./Generals were surprised by something they didn't know about.

CHECK-UP 5

1. Conversations between each pair will vary. (a) Pitcher: colonial woman who brought water to soldiers during a battle; Brant: Mohawk widow of Sir William Johnson who fought for Great Britain (b) Washington: wife of George Washington, who joined her husband at the front; Adams: wife of John Adams, who asked her husband to work for women's equality (c) Lafayette: French military officer who fought with the Americans; Steuben: German military officer who trained the American army (d) Burgoyne: general who led British troops at Saratoga; Gates: general who led American troops at Saratoga

2. (a) port and major colonial city held by British during Revolution (b) site of battle in which an entire British Army surrendered to Americans; turning point of the war (c) Terrible winter camp at which Americans were trained by von Steuben and developed spirit to win war (d) George Rogers Clark won battles that gave temporary control of Ohio to Americans and frustrated British plans.

3. Responses will vary.

4. Possible response: The Revolution was a "people's war" because so many of the American people were in favor of it and fought in it. Women, children, and slaves fought. Ordinary citizens became soldiers. The spirit of Valley Forge gave the army courage.

5. (a) I too wanted equality. (b) I was a powder boy aboard a ship and was captured by the British. (c) I would not betray my country, and I went to jail with other Patriots.

6. Lafayette gave military help; Salomon gave financial help.

7. The British moved too slowly through the wilderness due to Americans resisting and blocking roads. Other armies did not come to Burgoyne's aid. The British ran out of supplies. At Saratoga, they were caught in a trap between the army led by General Gates and sharp-shooting farmers, and had to surrender.

8. Washington led his men to victory in battle; his dignity and manner made the soldiers devoted to him; in hard times, he suffered with his men and kept his army together.

9. After Saratoga, the French came into the war on the American side. They brought supplies and military might, which helped the Americans win the war.

10. *Lafayette:* France; 19-year-old nobleman; wanted to avenge father's death, believed in liberty Americans were fighting for. *Forten:* America; 14-year-old free African American, son of a sailmaker; believed in liberty and his country. *Kosciuszko:* Poland; young nobleman who owned an estate with serfs; trying to forget a girl he loved, believed in liberty. *Salomon:* Poland; educated businessman; wanted religious freedom and believed in liberty. All four of these people were willing to fight or work for liberty.

CHECK-UP 6

1. (a) *Cornwallis:* general who led British troops at Yorktown; *Clinton:* commander in chief of British forces in America; Clinton was Cornwallis's boss. (b) *De Grasse:* commander of French fleet that kept the British fleet from relieving British forces at Yorktown. (c) *Rochambeau and Washington:* French general and American general who joined forces to surround and defeat British at Yorktown. (d) *Lafayette, Steuben, and Wayne:* military leaders who joined Rochambeau and Washington at Yorktown.

2. (a) Spanish were building missions and solidifying their hold to ward off advances by Russians. (b) The Northwest Ordinance prepared this territory for statehood.

3. (a) The power of the government was divided into three branches—executive, legislative, and judicial—so that they balanced each other and kept each other in check. (b) The government could not proclaim an official religion, and so could not force people to practice a certain religion.

4. (a) Goddard printed the first copies of the Declaration of Independence. (b) She would not tell who the author was of articles she printed. (c) She worked at jobs that were usually men's work. (d) She freed her slave and gave her property to her former slave.

5. (a) Small states had the same voting power as large states. (b) The government could not collect taxes to run the government. (c) The government could not build an army. (d) Citizens felt more loyalty to their states than to a nation.

6. It was the first time territories would become states in a fair way, equal with the older states.

7. (a) Georgia, Virginia, Massachusetts, New York, Connecticut (b) Ohio, Illinois, Indiana, Michigan, Wisconsin, and part of Minnesota (c) freedom of religion, *habeas corpus*, trial by jury, no slavery, establishment of public schools

8. Responses will vary, but should include Jefferson's important achievements.

9. (a) The states argued over borders and taxes; they loosely united under the Articles of Confederation. (b) Native Americans fought settlers who wanted their land; the Native Americans lost, and their way of life was destroyed. (c) The state government wanted to control people's beliefs; Jefferson wrote the Statute for Religious Freedom and got it passed, ending state control of religious beliefs.

10. Students label Ohio, Illinois, Indiana, Michigan, Wisconsin, and Minnesota.

CHECK-UP 7

1. He organized the Constitutional Convention, he studied hard and brought to the convention a knowledge of government, he wrote the Virginia Plan, he took notes that tell us what happened at the convention meetings, and he wrote the Bill of Rights.

2. Responses will vary.

3. (a) a government made up of a group of partners; Framers who did not want a strong central government liked the idea of a confederation. (b) a government that divides power between a central government and state governments; Framers who wanted a strong central government liked the idea of a federation. (c) lawmaking body; one branch of the new government (d) government's leader, such as a president; another branch of the new government (e) court system; third branch of the new government (f) two parts of the legislature; balanced power among large and small states (g) addition to the Constitution; the only way the Constitution can be changed (h) To approve; the states had to approve the Constitution before it could become the law of the land.

4. Responses will vary, but should include the guarantee of human rights and freedom, self-government through representatives, and a system that keeps the branches of government from gaining too much power.

5. The Virginia Plan said that the number of congressmen from a state should be based on its population. The New Jersey Plan said all states should have the same number of congressmen.

6. The Great Compromise solved the problem of how big and small states would be represented in Congress. It said there should be two houses of the legislature. The Senate would have two representatives from each state.

Representation in the House of Representatives would be based on the population of each state.

7. (a) Slavery is morally wrong and inhumane. (b) Southern planters depend on slavery. (c) To get all the states to accept the Constitution, slavery would have to be allowed for a while.

8. Mason believed that the Constitution was not good enough and that it should have outlawed slavery. Henry wanted powerful states, not a powerful central government.

9. compromise over how large and small states are represented; compromise over slavery; compromise over the powers and form of the three branches of government

10. *Native American:* Doesn't include me, since the white settlers are taking my lands and breaking their treaties. *Woman:* Doesn't include me, since I can't vote and am not considered a citizen. *Slave:* Doesn't include me, since I am considered to be property and don't have human rights.

RESOURCE 1
Question Chart for use throughout the book.

RESOURCE 2
1. 1750 map: British—13 colonies British; French—all of the territory west of the Appalachians and Canada; Spanish—Florida

2. 1763 map: British—13 colonies, territory west of the Appalachians to the Mississippi, and Canada; Spanish—Florida and territory west of the Mississippi

RESOURCE 3
1. Franklin thinks the ties between the colonies and England are very close. He calls the colonies "sons" and England "the mother." He says England is still "our pride" and that the colonies will fight on England's side.

2. Students may predict that the colonies and Britain might separate and even become enemies. Some clues are Amherst's attitude toward Johnson and Native Americans; Britain's belief that the Americans should help pay for the war; and the movement of settlers into Indian lands, which Britain tried to prevent.

3. Responses will vary.

RESOURCE 4
Students' bar graphs should correspond to the figures in the table.

RESOURCE 5
1. *World Book Encyclopedia; Encyclopedia of Black America;* Josiah Henson

2. The author uses words such as *my, we,* and *our.*

3. Possible response: The advantages of the primary source include it is an eyewitness report and it makes the reader feel as if he or she is at the event. The advantages of the secondary source includes that it combines information from many sources and gives the reader a general picture of the event.

RESOURCE 6
Chart—Adams: a busybody who got everyone else excited; lost family money; Boston; stirred up colonists against British and began Committes of Correspondence. Paine: writer; had many jobs that didn't work out; Philadelphia; wrote *Common Sense,* wrote "These are the times that try men's souls." Henry: great speaker; failed at being a storekeeper and planter; Virginia; attacked the Stamp Act and said "give me liberty or give me death!"

1. The colonies should break away from England.

2. Responses will vary.

RESOURCE 7
1. approximately 900 miles

2. Massachusetts, Connecticut, New York, New Jersey, Pennsylvania, Delaware, Maryland, Virginia, North Carolina, South Carolina

3. about 5 days

4. about 36 days

RESOURCE 8
1. Lee **2.** Franklin **3.** Jefferson **4.** Hopkins **5.** Rush **6.** Hewes **7.** Washington; students' puzzles will vary.

RESOURCE 9
1. The British outnumber the Americans.

2. approximately 4,000 feet

3. Students should draw a line from Charles River around Morton's Point to Charlestown Neck, or from the river to the Causeway where troops could then march to the Neck. It was lucky for the Americans because they were able to escape through the Neck.

RESOURCE 10
1. Possible response: He thinks it will get out of hand. Words such as *no end to it* and *demand* indicate he is worried about what might happen if everyone wanted independence.

2. Responses will vary.

3. Responses will vary.

RESOURCE 11

1. 632,300
2. 4,440
3. 6,188
4. 189,372
5. $150,000,000 each year

RESOURCE 12

1. e **2.** a **3.** f **4.** c **5.** b **6.** d **7.** Responses will vary.

RESOURCE 13

1. York River, James River; Chesapeake Bay
2. The British navy could supply and protect his troops from the sea.
3. about 500 miles; about 12.5 miles a day
4. The French navy defeated the British navy at Chesapeake Bay. There was no help for the British army after it was surrounded by the American and French forces.

RESEARCH 14

1. author of the Declaration of Independence; author of the Virginia Statute of Religious Freedom; father of the University of Virginia
2. Responses will vary, and may include playing the violin, being elected governor of Virginia, being elected president of the United States.
3. Possible response: He did not free his slaves.
4. Responses will vary.

RESOURCE 15

Part I: 1. Article I, Section 2 **2.** Article I, Section 3 **3.** Article I, Section 8 **4.** Article II, Section 1 **5.** Article II, Section 2 **6.** Article III, Section 2 **7.** Article IV, Section 3 **8.** Article V, Section 9 **9.** Article VI **10.** Article VII
Part II: 1. state **2.** national **3.** national **4.** national **5.** state **6.** state

Printed in the USA
CPSIA information can be obtained
at www.ICGtesting.com
CBHW081038040224
3957CB00009B/18

9 780199 767366